T0114657

IMPETUS
MIND

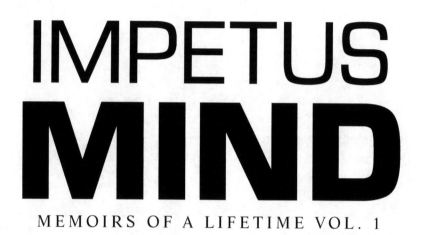

IMPETUS MIND

MEMOIRS OF A LIFETIME VOL. 1

JERROD BIGLOW

To order additional copies of this book, contact:
Xlibris
844-714-8691
www.Xlibris.com
Orders@Xlibris.com
856473

Contents

"Out beyond ideas of wrongdoing and right doing there is a field. I'll meet you there. When the soul lies down in that grass the world is too full to talk about"

Rumi

"I've spent many days plus numerous nights wondering about my lot in life, looking within myself for clues to a question that has left me perplexed for many decades. I've often contemplated for hours questioning if there is a divine design for my life."

Jerrod A. Biglow

"There are seven dominant spheres of influence: movies, music, television, books, the internet, law, and family. The tier of influences are schools, peers, newspapers, radio and business".

George Barna

"It's not the critic who counts; not the man who points out how the strong man stumbles, or where the doer of deeds could have done better. The credit belongs to the man who is actually in the arena… Who at best knows in the end the triumph of great achievements, and who at worst, if he fails, at least fails while daring greatly. So that his place will never be with those cold timid souls who know neither victory nor defeat".

Theodore Roosevelt

"I Believe with all my heart that each and every one of us has been given unique gifts from the creator and that each one of us has been called to apply those gifts to a purpose in life"

Dani Johnson

"We didn't give ourselves the personalities, talents, or longings we were born with. When we fulfill these – these gifts from beyond ourselves – it is like fulfilling something we were meant to do…. The Creator of all things knows the name of each of us – knows thoroughly, better than we do ourselves, what is in us, for he put it there and intends for us to do something with it – something that meshes with his intentions for many other people…. Even if we do not always think of it that way, each of us was given a calling – by fate, by chance, by destiny, by God.

Those who are lucky have found it"

Michael Novak

"As the dusk darkened the always shadowed Sistine chapel, Michelangelo, weary, sore and doubtful, climbed down the ladder from his scaffolding where he'd been lying on his back since dawn painting the chapel ceiling. After eating a lonely dinner, he wrote a sonnet to his aching body. The last line [was]…. I'm no painter but when the sun shone again, Michelangelo got up from his bed, climbed up his scaffold, and labored another day on his magnificent vision of the creator."

Lewis Smedes

There comes a time in a man's life where he evaluates current circumstances while evaluating and internalizing his options that would put him in the arena he was born for. Looking at life from a seed time and harvest perspective we gain an understanding of conducive seasons and advantageous environments. Learning when to plant our seeds and when to water is critical to our growth. A person's seed is their innate talents and gifts. The water provided during the dormant stage in which ushers a seed into its fruitful season is the time invested. All the seasons in between are period in life which teaches of us patience and gives understanding as we retrospect. The dry season in life teaches us to at times, accept situations for what they truly are that are outside our ability to change. On the other hand, giving us experience with speaking into exigent situations we face to bring about a desired outcome. There have been times in my life where I was perplexed and allowed myself to be boxed in or placed in a setting where I had no control over the outcome. I would sit and wish that it were possible to turn back the hands of time. Since no one is given a supernatural ability to manipulate time and space we must use our most valuable resource valiantly. In Leadership Qualities: Steward Dr. Kenneth Boa wrote Consider for a moment that everyone on earth has the same amount of time in every day. President or paper boy, housewife or executive, farmer or financier – they all have exactly 24 hours in each day, 168 hours in each week, 525,600 minutes in each year. Some people take that time and build relationships, dream dreams and make plans, cultivate their walk with God, develop new skills and live lives of adventure. We must govern how our time is spent, evaluate, strategically plan, and visualize where life's many roads could potentially lead us to remain on course to fulfill our destiny.

"If there is one lesson in life that I have learned it is this:
You never know when your life is about to change. You
never know when one decision will dramatically impact
your life and change the course of your destiny."
Dani Johnson

I've heard a saying: "we live forward and understand our experiences backwards." At the moment of conception, we're giving 23 chromosomes from each parent. The x or y factor is what determines the gender. The man's seed produced during copulation is the life force that ushers' one generation into the next. We may not understand the reason why we are so passionate about a particular topic or adamant about the way we feel regarding certain fields. The answer may be found in an experience or even a conversation had by our parents or grandparents. When looking to cultivate our best we ensure that the best seed is planted in the most fertile ground. Everyone in agriculture knows that the seed is only as fruitful as the soil allows it to be. I've come to an understanding that life itself is a process of selection. To obtain the most out of life one must be very selective concerning the choices we make and who we choose to spend our lives with. The one thing that separates mankind from every other social genius of animals is our ability to use what we know as the mind. The human mind is continuously developing and evolving consciously and unconsciously. Our understanding of existence, the law of attraction, spiritual and natural laws continue to expand parallels with our experiences and research. Many studies have been conducted pertaining to simultaneous thoughts, actions, events, and consciousness.

Carl Jung coined the phenomenon synchronicity. Which is the coincidental occurrence of events and especially psychic events (such as similar thoughts in widely separated persons or a mental image of an unexpected event before it happens) that seem related but are not explained by conventional mechanisms of causality. Because the subject matter was poorly researched and defined, many modern psychologists have shied away from the ideology. Though unproven Carl Jung's studies add validity in the importance of enveloping yourself in the right body. Very little research has been directed toward the understanding of the pineal gland's abilities and functions.

Some believe it has a direct connection with spiritual awareness and psychic abilities. There are many writings and studies regarding the development and changes of the pineal gland such as "Materials and Methods" which is a retrospective autopsy study of 72 pediatric and adult cases, "The Jerusalem Stone of Consciousness", and "The Pineal Gland: Eye of the God", to name a few. Studies suggest the stimulation of the vagus nerve increases the activity of the gland while ingesting some minerals such as fluoride and other chemicals has the opposite effect shrinking and calcifying the pineal gland. Some even believe the quality of communication we digest is just as important as the tangible sustenance we take in. The company that we become dissolved in usually persuades our vision, perception, and the way we see life through our own eyes and perception of the mind.

"The most pathetic person in the world is
someone who has sight but no vision"
Helen Keller

As we learn to understand life through a broader spectrum the fruits of our labor that we manifest become more advantageous to producing a full and meaningful life. We've all seen infomercials that claim to make our lives less challenging only to find out the product was sold off a meaningless marketing scheme. (In my opinion, life wasn't given for us to necessarily have an easy life. Life is an experience that each one of us unconsciously breeched while given a unique code passed down in order to fill a void.) Life is an experience meant for us to embrace as significant stewards of our environment mentally and tangibly. Humanity consciously seeks to find ways to pursue happiness and make life more livable and fulfilling. With all the conscience efforts, society is still on a parallel course guided in a direction of degradation of human consciousness. Scholars suggest that there was once a time when ancient civilizations could move matter by sound and thought alone. A true mark of science erudition. In our era many auspicious inventions have come along. None of the magnitude of our ancient ancestors. If there was true progression in human consciousness mankind would have more of an understanding for the blueprints to sustaining life. Some of the most ingenious minds and brilliant people to ever manifest comprehensible breakthroughs in this lifetime have only created destruction and chaos. Albert Einstein for example, outside of the formula E=mc2, his greatest brainchild was a weapon of mass destruction the atom bomb. As we move to a more complex world it seems many of the populous around the world is losing the ability to conjure the simplest cognitive abilities. Something like owning ten cars with only excess to drive one. This is simply a metaphor describing the capacity and potential humans possess to facilitate the full ability of our brains. Science suggests that humans on average use only 10% of our brains. Imagine what life would be like if we possessed the ability to excess at least half or the brains full capacity. I'm certain humanity would experience the power to appreciate one another on a higher resonant level.

The linguistics we use to communicate plays a major role in how we respond, our body language, and how we encode and decode. Envision our ability to communicate as a highway and the flow of traffic as the understanding amongst patrons. A two-lane highway can't handle the same amount of traffic that a 4-lane highway can during peak traveling hours. What was efficient during one period may be obsolete during another. The vehicle used to project information in today's era equips us with the ability to be globally aware. Our minds form a web as we connect, interact, and share thoughts. I like to think of that web as an intellectual grid that can push images and information at the speed of an electrical impulse. Imagine if you had the privilege to be involved in daily discourse with some of today's most sought-after minds how that dialogue would affect your mental evolution if you were able to digest the information. If the learned came together and challenged one another mentally exercising the mind's ability as if it were a bicep the small body of individuals would meta morph into a think tank that I call the impetus mind. Rome used a strategic method when going into battle. Thousands of men would train to fight as a single moving unit. Many prospect soldiers, I'm sure may have been denied the right to serve as a roman soldier due to their inability to move in sync with their fellow comrade. For example, in the movie 300 king Leonidas denies one of his soldiers the right to continue fighting because he sustained an injury that impeded his vision. Life is a lot like that movie. When a group of individuals are on the same level of consciousness and share linear thinking, the possibilities to accomplish any goal is limitless. When brilliant, intuitive, and insightful people enjoin with open minds and quintessential ideas the volume of accountability, discipline, integrity and brainpower is insatiable. In the Republic, Plato talks about an ideal number of citizens in his time that would make up an ideal society. The right number along with the proper talents is essential. Too many of even the right people can create an unproductive environment.

Plato's theory is a lot like synergy the interaction or cooperation of two or more organizations, substances, or other agents that produce a combined effect greater than the sum of their separate effects. So, in life it's a rule of thumb to connect with those with similar vision. This ideology is where the old saying comes from the whole is greater than the sum of its parts. When we begin to understand as well as respect the capacity of space and time we have for a certain number of people in our lives the people we choose to share our lives with will be patrons. Life is art displayed on the corridor of a timeline. So, when you choose to share your art with those who are willing to open, accept and become vulnerable to your gifted expression make an earnest decision based on things beyond a superficial nature in a tangible world. People tend to gravitate to situations and other individuals that add to their lives and are advantageous to personal growth. Yet many of us often overlook personal growth as removing yourself from a situation or person. Sometimes subtraction truly is addition. Growth is a natural part of life which increases our hunger to validate new hopes with success which in turns feeds confidence that grows within and sparks new fires deep within an earnest man who is honest with himself. As we all know, fires spread with seeming ease with the right components. When communication is properly encoded and decoded, we digest each other's thoughts and intellectual property building an inner working of shared consciousness creating one mind that becomes more than a think tank but a web like vortex operating on neurological programing that's progressive to moving in the direction of any sought objective.

Humans thrive on communication, especially positive affirmation. Masaru Emoto discovered that even crystals reveal specific changes when concentrated thoughts are directed towards them. His studies reveal that water from clean springs and water exposed to positive affirmations show brilliant, complex, and colorful snowflake patterns. While positive affirmation had a positive affect on the geometric form of the frozen water crystals negative thoughts and words had a negative effect on the natural harmonious geometric symmetry of the water. You may ask why this is important. The answer is the human body is comprised of 70% water. This is why it's important to surround yourself with the right people. I think the most effective way to surround yourself with pupils would be to start small. As I mentioned earlier. In Plato's Republic he touches base on the ideal number of citizens for an ideal city-state. His ideology is a formula for a healthy government. Even though his Socratic dialogue was based on a larger scale it can be scaled down to work on a personal level. Many believed that Plato was ahead of his time. This may be the reason that many of his ideas are still relevant in even today's society. Plato's ideas influenced how people looked at justice, population control and norms within a society. Plato's idea that resonates with me mostly is his belief in how the many facets of a city-state come together as a conglomerate. Many times, we often miss the true identity of a society as a whole due to being blinded by the fabrics of life that we haven't experienced or because we are programmed by what we have experienced. We've all heard the saying "can't see the forest because of the trees". Many overlook connections linked to our destinations and purposes in life because normally the connection is not familiar to us. One of the many reasons is that in this day in age our eyes and hearts are never satisfied for material gain. This intoxicating insatiable thirst for the innumerable desires of men causes many of us to only focus on the things we believe will get us ahead in life. The drawback to one navigating through life with a mentality of only putting forth one's energy toward the people, places or things that we assume will further our journey in the direction thought to be best. No one knows the beginning from the end. Leaving many of us blind to the true essence of the law of attraction. Inevitably leaving us off balanced and drained rather than being well rounded. When selflessness is what drives our thoughts and actions, we find that our goals and desires are usually linked to other like-minded individuals willing to assist us in the direction that destiny has called us to go.

In The bible the wise are instructed to guard their heart because out of the heart flows the issues of life proverb 4:23. It's also advised to be vigilant keeping watch with a sound mind 1 peter 5:8. The heart and the mind are the two most important facets of life. This is why mind heart coherence is important. Desire begins in the heart while manifestation begins in the mind. Our thoughts are cultivated from the dimension of one's imagination. Synthetic imagination is the faculty that allows us to arrange old concepts, ideas, or plans into new combinations. Synthetic imagination creates nothing alone. It uses past experiences, education, and observation with which it is fed. It is the faculty used most by the inventor or creator with the exception of the one who draws upon the creative imagination, when one cannot solve his or her problem through synthetic imagination. Creative imagination is where the finite mind of man directs communication with infinite intelligence. It is the dimension through which hunches and inspirations are received. It is by this faculty that all basic, or new ideas are handed over to man. Imagine mankind before we possessed the ability to speak and associate sounds with meaning in order to communicate. Man would have to obtain an understanding amongst one another with different means. How we encode and decode determines the effectiveness of our communication. As we build and grow surrounding ourselves with people that embrace the way we feel about life and share many of our own ideologies and thoughts our circumstances around us begin to reflect the propensity of energy which resonates within us. As one takes an inventory of him or herself, we may discover during these times the law of subtraction overlaps with the law of addition. Subtraction is defined simply as the art of removing anything excessive, confusing, wasteful, unnatural, hazardous, hard to use, or ugly or the discipline to refrain from adding it in the first place. When a person removes anything that impedes progress, anything that is hazardous, or is ugly we add value to our own lives consequentially adding value to those around us. As people learn to become selfless, we gain an understanding that by placing another's pre-potent needs before our own, we begin to place ourselves in the arena of a leading man or woman.

"Perception doesn't accomplish goals; substance
does. Know who you really are and where you
are going, and then pursue your goals."
Tony Dungy

These are quotes by one of the most famous leading men to walk the face of the earth.

Martin Lurther King Statues:

- "Out of the mountain of despair, a stone of hope."
- "I was a drum major for justice, peace and righteousness."
- "We shall overcome because the arc of the moral universe is long, but it bends toward justice."
- "Darkness cannot drive out darkness, only light can do that."
- "Injustice anywhere is a threat to justice everywhere."
- "Our lives begin to end the day we become silent about things that matter."
- "One day we will learn that the heart can never be totally right when the head is totally wrong."

(Martin Lurther King stuck his head up in a time when it was dangerous to do so. The 60's was a very prejudice time. In his era, he voiced that it was the content of a person's heart rather than the complexion of their skin that determine their character and equity. This is a true archetype of a leading man. Not because his walk was unblemished but because his cause and deeds were selfless.)

John Maxwell's 21 laws of leadership:

1. **The Law of the Lid Leadership** Ability Determines a Person's Level of Effectiveness Brothers Dick and Maurice came as close as they could to living the American Dream— without making it. Instead, a guy named Ray did it with the company they had founded. It happened because they didn't know the Law of the Lid.

2. **The Law of Influence** The true Measure of Leadership Is Influence—Nothing More, Nothing Less Her husband had everything: wealth, privilege, position, and a royal title. Yet instead of him, Princess Diana won over the whole world. Why? She understood the Law of Influence.

3. **The Law of Process** Leadership Develops Daily, not in a Day Theodore Roosevelt helped create a world power, won a Nobel Peace Prize, and became president of the United States. But today you wouldn't even know his name if he hadn't known the Law of Process.

4. **The Law of Navigation** Anyone Can Steer the Ship, But It Takes a Leader to Chart the Course Using a fail-safe compass, Scott led his team of adventurers to the end of the earth—and to inglorious deaths. They would have lived if only he, their leader, had known the Law of Navigation.

5. **The Law of E. F. Hutton** When the Real Leader Speaks, People Listen Young John went into his first board meeting

thinking he was in charge. He soon found out who the real leader was and learned the Law of E. F. Hutton in the process.

6. **The Law of Solid Ground** Trust Is the Foundation of Leadership If only Robert McNamara had known the Law of Solid Ground, the War in Vietnam—and everything that happened at home because of it—might have turned out differently.

7. **The Law of Respect** People Naturally Follow Leaders Stronger Than Themselves The odds were stacked against her in just about every possible way, but thousands and thousands of people called her their leader. Why? Because they could not escape the power of the Law of Respect.

8. **The Law of Intuition** Leaders Evaluate Everything with a Leadership Bias How is it that time after time Norman Schwarzkopf was able to sense problems while other leaders around him got blindsided? The answer lies in the factor that separates the great leaders from the merely good ones: the Law of Intuition.

9. **The Law of Magnetism** Who You Are Is Who You Attract Why are the Dallas Cowboys, once revered as "America's Team," now so often reviled and the subject of controversy? The Law of Magnetism makes it clear.

10. **The Law of Connection** Leaders Touch a Heart Before They Ask for a Hand Elizabeth Dole has mastered it. If husband

Bob had done the same, he might have become the forty-third president of the United States. It's called the Law of Connection.

11. **The Law of the Inner Circle** A Leader's Potential Is Determined by Those Closest to Him. John already used time management to the fullest, but he wanted to accomplish more. His priorities were already leveraged to the hilt, and there were no more minutes in a day! How did he go to a new level? He practiced the Law of the Inner Circle.

12. **The Law of Empowerment** Only Secure Leaders Give Power to Others Henry Ford is considered an icon of American business for revolutionizing the automobile industry. So, what caused him to stumble so badly that his son feared Ford Motor Company would go out of business? He was held captive by the Law of Empowerment.

13. **The Law of Reproduction** (It Takes a Leader to Raise Up a Leader) What do the top NFL head coaches have in common? You can trace their leadership ability to just a handful of mentors. That's also true for hundreds of CEOs. More than 80 percent of all leaders are the result of the Law of Reproduction.

14. **The Law of Buy-In** People Buy into the Leader, Then the Vision The first time Judy Estrim started up a company, it took her six months to find the money. The second time it

took her about six minutes. What made the difference? The Law of Buy In.

15. **The Law of Victory** Leaders Find a Way for the Team to Win What saved England from the Blitz, broke apartheid's back in South Africa, and won the Chicago Bulls multiple world championships? In all three cases the answer is the same. Their leaders lived by the Law of Victory.

16. **The Law of the Big Mo** Momentum Is a Leader's Best Friend Jaime Escalante has been called the best teacher in America. But his teaching ability is only half the story. His and Garfield High School's success came because of the Law of the Big Mo.

17. **The Law of Priorities** Leaders Understand that Activity Is Not Necessarily Accomplishment Jack Welch took a company that was already flying high and rocketed it into the stratosphere. What did he use as the launching pad? The Law of Priorities, of course.

18. **The Law of Sacrifice** A Leader Must Give Up to Go Up He was one of the nation's most vocal critics on government interference in business. So why did Lee Iacocca go before Congress with his hat in his hand for loan guarantees? He did it because he understood the Law of Sacrifice.

19. **The Law of Timing** When to Lead Is as Important as What to Do and Where to Go It got him elected president of the United States. It also cost him the presidency. What is it?

Something that may stand between you and your ability to lead effectively. It's called the Law of Timing.

20. **The Law of Explosive Growth** To Add Growth, Lead Followers—To Multiply, Lead Leaders How did a man in a developing country take his organization from 700 people to more than 14,000 in only seven years? He did it using leader's math. That's the secret of the Law of Explosive Growth.

21. **The Law of Legacy** (A Leader's Lasting Value Is Measured by Succession) When many companies lose their CEO, they go into a tailspin. But when Roberto Goizueta died, Coca-Cola didn't even hiccup. Why? Before his death, Goizueta lived by the Law of Legacy.

Al Ries and Jack Trout's 22 Immutable laws of marketing

1. **Law of Leadership**. Being first in the market is better than having a better product.

2. **Law of category**. It's hard to gain leadership in a category with a lot of competition. It's better to create a new category.

3. **Law of mind**. It's not important to be first in the market but first in the mind of consumers. One way to get mind-share is out advertise earlier competitor.

4. **Law of perception**. Marketing is not about products but about perceptions. What we call reality is just a perception of reality that we create in our minds.

5. **Law of focus**. The most powerful concept in marketing is owning a word in the prospect's mind. Owning in this context means that if people hear or see this word, they usually connect it with a company that "owns" the word.

6. **Law of exclusivity**. It's fruitless to try to take over a word that is already owned by a competitor.

7. **Law of the ladder**. Marketing strategy depends on your position in the market.

8. **Law of duality**. In the long run every market becomes a two-horse race.

9. **Law of opposite**. If you're shooting for second place your strategy is determined by the leader. Leverage the leader's

strength into a weakness. Don't try to be better than the leader, try to be different.

10. **Law of Division**. Over time a category will split into two or more categories.

11. **Law of perspective**. Marketing effects take place over an extended period of time. It's a mistake to sacrifice long term planning with actions that improve short term balance sheets.

12. **Law of extension**. There's an irresistible pressure to extend the equity of the brand and it's a mistake. Instead, one should create new brands to address new markets/products.

13. **Law of sacrifice**. You have to give up something in order to get something. There are three things to sacrifice. Product line, target market, and constant change.

14. **Law of Attributes**. For every attribute there is an opposite effective attribute. You can't own the same word as the competition. You have to find another word to own, another attribute.

15. **Law of candor**. When you admit a negative, the prospect will give you a positive. Candor is disarming. It's ok to admit.

16. **Law of singularity**. In each situation only one move will produce substantial results. In marketing the only thing that works is a single bold stroke.

17. **Law of predictability**. Unless you write your competitors plans you can't predict the future. You don't know the future, you don't know what your competition will do so you have to build

your company and marketing strategies to be flexible, to be able to quickly respond to changing situations.

18. **Law of success**. Success often leads to arrogance, and arrogance to failure.

19. **Law of failure**. Failure is to be expected and accepted. Drop things that don't work instead of fixing them. Don't punish for failures because if you do people will stop taking risks.

20. **Law of hype**. The situation is often the opposite of the way it appears in the press. The amount of hype isn't proportional to success. Often failed products are heavily hyped.

21. **Law of acceleration**. Successful programs are not built on fads but on trends.

22. **Law of resources**. Without adequate funding an idea won't get off the ground.

Plato's dialogue on philosophical ideas, Ethics, Metaphysics, and platonic love display thoughts far ahead of their time and in time became the subject matter for institutional learning influencing Aristotle and many others who were personally selected to glean from his thoughts and ideas. Plato's The Republic is one of those dialogues that is considered a Socratic dialogue outlining the fabrics of order as well as the characteristics of a just city state and a just man. The first book of Plato dissects justice. He gave humanity a clear aspect of how true justice should be practiced.

In contrast, Plato teaches us that we should be selective in who we allow in our governments, student bodies, communities, companies, think tanks and private groups. To take it a step further, it's just as important to be selective regarding what a person allows in their receptive gates. We should personally select those around us and what we receive and are receptive to just as Plato was very selective when choosing his student body. Plato gives us an archetype of true justice and a just man. Having a representation of that archetype is enabling through the model of what he describes as true justice.

A story of Socrates:

While visiting Piraeus with Glaucon, Polemarchus tells Socrates to join him for a romp. Socrates then asks Cephalus, Polemarchus, and Thrasymachus their definitions of justice. Cephalus defines justice as giving what is owed. Polemarchus says justice is "the art which gives good to friends and evil to enemies." Thrasymachus proclaims "justice is nothing else than the interest of the stronger." Socrates overturns their definitions and says that it is to your advantage to be just and disadvantage to be unjust. He also elaborates on the facets of government and the laws there of. He states that each particular Government make laws for their own interest and the laws are considered justice passed down underhanded to its citizens. Whoever breaks those laws are considered to be unjust and tried in an atrium ratio known to as the court system and judged by a magistrate.

"The land scape of your future is in large part determined by what you think it will be and by how you see yourself in it. For better or worse, what you envision often begins to take shape. Be intentional and choose to envision a life of significance, possibility and impact"
Tony Dungy

In today's society it is very easy to get caught up in the ways of the modern world. Our hearts and eyes tend to never be satisfied. We intoxicate our judgment not only by consuming alcohol but also with the lust of the flesh. At times many of us feel like all the things we yearn for, and value come in tangible packages. Which causes many to fall short when it comes to fruits of the spirit. Many years ago, I read a quote "never take down a fence until you know what it is keeping out or in". I believe that's how it was written. Today, in a microwave society we are all too quick to remove boundaries before we know the purpose they serve. Though it may be true what worked yesterday may be obsolete today. We must understand a lot of knowledge and wisdom have been lost over the ages. New doesn't always equate to superior or indicate relevancy. With all the technology scientists have at their disposal we're still trying to figure out how the great pyramids of Giza were built. How ancient civilizations moved large, quarried stones and constructed some of the wonders of the world. For example, The temple of Artemis, The lighthouse of Alexandria, Mausoleum at Halicarnassus and Stonehenge. Some modern scientists believe that what modern society call a primitive society possessed a lost understanding of sound that moved or lightened the weight of a load to make it possible to construct many of the feats that still have mankind perplexed today. Scientists call it harmonics, cymatics, and levitation by sound. Some believe everything owes its existence to sound. The Pandora box opened has left this civilization stripped of many gifts on a metaphysical and spiritual level because of thirst for pleasures and the misconception of wants versus needs. As "wants" turns to "needs" in the aspect of norms for a society many enlightened intellectuals lights grow dim. The transcending effects are passed down from generation to generation, as a trade off losing one ability to gain another. For example, habitual use of a cell phone alleviates the ability to retain and memorize certain information. I remember growing up how I would go to the movies with my friends and see a girl of interest. I would approach her and if I was lucky enough to say the right thing, I would walk away with a phone number tucked away in my cerebral cortex. Now the chances of me remembering a lady's phone number are like the odds of the Tyson- Buster Douglas fight. Which leaves me with a rhetorical question: are we getting further from our goals and purpose and closer to an oasis? I think the better question for modern society would be: what are our goals? Is it just mere existence and survival? I've noticed a growing trend of how the masses appoint a selected few to delegate and solve problems for us all. Then when the few pushes an agenda that's distasteful or unpopular they are martyred for their beliefs. In the 20's through the 60's there was a saying "it takes us all". That way of thinking has faded along with other morals as well. As I mentioned earlier, decisions we make in life either bring us closer to the arena you and I were built for or push us further away leaving us by the wayside hoping to get in the game. As the saying goes, you reap what you sow. If you go around planting apple seeds don't expect pomegranates.

"your vision will become clear only when you look into your heart. Who looks outside, dreams; who looks inside awakens"

Carl Jung

"A leader will find it difficult to articulate a coherent vision unless it expresses his core values, & his basic identity. One must first embark on the formidable journey of self-discovery in order to create a vision with the authentic soul."

Mihaley Csikszentmihalyi

Representation is often best displayed by someone who has a clear understanding of who and what they are representing. Allowing the right person to represent you in the right season could change the rest of your life. You don't need everyone to be for you just the right person or people. So many fail to realize the difference between confidants, constituents, and comrades. A confidant is a person you trust and able to share your most inner secrets with. A Constituent is nothing more than being part of a group. An example of a constituent could be anyone in your age group or generation. While a comrade is someone who may share your values as well as beliefs and shares a common goal or agenda with you. Everyone that enters your life will normally fall in one of these three categories. Most of the people we meet are just associates or constituents. You would be considered lucky to have more than 4 confidants in a lifetime. A confidant could come in the form of a teacher, cousin, friend or even a business partner. I remember listening to a motivational speaker years ago talk about how he and a partner entered a business venture together. The startup wasn't successful. He mentioned the partnership was right, the timing was right, but everything fell apart because he was in the wrong field.

If a farmer was trying to grow oranges in Nebraska in the middle of December, he would run into a similar situation. Everything we do in life has a time and a place. Anyone in business will advise business is approximately 80% location. As conscience beings we must be aware not just of who we are around but what we are around as well. Good seed also requires good ground.

A person's true calling is always tied to their deepest interest. Kevin Brennfleck who is a life calling coach states, "before being called to something, we are called to someone. Before being called to do we are called to be". Most times the answers that we are looking for lies deep within ourselves and around us we just must be willing to look. Some people look for answers while others search for problems. The one looking for problems could easily be considered confrontational or combative. Yet both parties are truly solution based. If we look at this with an analytical eye from a mathematician standpoint we may reevaluate. In math, addition the problem is presented, and one must find the answer. In Algebra the answer is giving, and one must find the missing part of the problem. In our quest to discover our calling and hidden talents we must look deep within ourselves for problems as well as solutions. One must take an honest inventory of himself as I mentioned earlier. When we search deep within ourselves, we discover our inner man. The spiritual and intellectual part of our existence. This discovery must be made. This is what Kevin Brennfleck is talking about when he mentions "before we are called to do, we are called to be". Into the depths of the inner man also known as the still voice within us we must retreat to hone the frequency and become fluent. Have you ever made a decision only to feel like you should have listened to that distinct voice crying out to you? We all have the ability to utilize our inner voice yet, many fail to train their inner ears to listen due to life's background noises within the hustle and bustle. Very few people feel like they have leisure time to take walks, meditate, or even focus on the seven types of rest (Physical, mental, emotional, sensory, creative, social, and spiritual) to rejuvenate. We've been trained to keep our feelings and emotions hidden in order to continue. As, a result our relationships take a hit in the quality department. I would compare these bad habits to the way the Government handles the national debt crisis. Never finding any real solutions to fix the crisis just stick a band aid on it for 40 days. It's okay to be optimistic and believe everything will normalize in the future. This tends to work from time to time. You have a disagreement that gets out of hand and some words were said that may have caused someone pain. It's true that time can heal, But when you find yourself feeling like Sisyphus going thru the same motion seeing the same results the only thing that comes to mind is Einstein. "Insanity is doing the same thing over and over and expecting different results". Often this is the reason so many individuals find themselves in groups, packs and cliques yet find themselves feeling alienated on the inside. Abraham Maslow gives an account of human motivation with the "Hierarchy of Needs". Maslow states at the heart of human actions is the desire to satisfy certain needs. At the base of the pyramid is the physiological level: breathing, food, water, sex, Sleep, homeostasis, and excretion. The next level is safety: security of body, of employment, of resources, of morality, of the family, of health, and of property. The third level is love-belonging: Friendship, family, and sexual intimacy. The fourth is Esteem: self-esteem, confidence, achievement, respect of others, and respect by others. The fifth and final level at the top is self-actualization: morality, creativity, spontaneity, problem solving, lack of prejudice, and acceptance of facts. This pyramid coined by Maslow gives a closer look to why many individuals find themselves in groups, relationships, and organizations that they don't really relate to. Humans have a desire of belonging. The true essence of a Group is intended to make us feel welcomed, safe and provide an atmosphere to socialize. So, when a person is affiliated with a group or person he or she can no longer relate to or has outgrown we tend to disassociate. Even if we are still physically present. Which is a disconnection and lack of continuity between thoughts, memories, surroundings, actions, and identity. The 4 stages of disassociation: First Mild detachment or daydreaming then moderate detachment including "spacing out" or "zoning out" next severe detachment or depersonalization where one feels disconnected from one's physical presence and last identity confusion, where an individual might not recognize themselves or their surroundings. If you find yourself feeling or behaving in this manner you should make it a priority to analyze your associations. Disassociation is not always an easy thing to deal with. Especially when the people who make you question your identity are coworkers, family, and friends. Too often we stifle our growth by tolerating people around us who refuse to mature, seek the truth, accept the truth, or not honest with you nor themselves, or just don't have any goals in life. Normally, when this shoe fits someone they would rather keep you from growing rather than growing themselves. We call this a crab in a bucket mentality. Some people have been programmed and are stuck in their own ways and will never believe one plus one has the combined ability to produce an effect greater than the sum of three. The power of cooperation or what is known as synergy gives clear understanding of what it truly means to "work together" with one another. I believe Henri Mazel was the first to apply this term to social psychology. In 1896 he wrote La Synergie

Sociale. He disagreed with Charles Darwin's theory on the account he overlooked social love what Mazel coined as "social synergy". A collective evolutionary drive. When we surround ourselves with those who truly have our interest in mind as well as their own the sky is the limit as far a what the mind can manifest. In any type of relationship that is healthy reciprocation must be practiced.

Relationships are like bank accounts. In order to make a withdrawal there also must be a deposit. Being mindful of the present allows a person to be more aware of their presence. Having a grasp of what's current perpetuates a path for your dominate self in the future. Being stuck in the past disrupts the present. Balance is essential. If we focus too much on the future, we lose sight of the moment. Losing sight of the moment cripples our ability to take the necessary steps to bridge the moment with the future we long for. On the other hand, if we constantly worry about where we are now normally, we become paralyzed with fear because the situation is rarely perfect or just how we would like it to be. A healthy plant requires certain elements in order to grow. The environment doesn't have to be perfect. Just certain resources must be in place and those resources must be balanced. If not, the plant will wilt and die. Looking back at Maslow's hierarchy he describes the elements required for a hominid to live a balanced life. Like trying to put a square peg in a circle hole, often many of us look to fit in parts of society we don't have the capacity to relate, or some feel they don't belong. Where do you go when you don't feel you belong due to certain beliefs, way of life, ways of thinking, ethnicity, or religion? Who has the right to decide who belongs? Who sets the standard or pattern in which our social behaviors are typically based and expected within society? All these are great questions that I can't answer for you. I can only answer them for myself. Just as you would have to answer them for yourself. When we begin to ask ourselves these questions, they become stimuli for thought of change for the better.

"Pushing through the fear is less frightening than living with the underlying fear that comes from a feeling of helplessness."
Susan Jeffers

The social structure currently in place is heavily influenced by monetary gain. We make many of our decisions based on money. We select our friends based off money. We choose who we will marry, or date based solely off money. As I study the financial system, I gain more understanding that the financial system is only a mere temporary belief system. You may wonder why I say temporary. Everything in life is transient. The currency that we use to settle our debts is considered fiat. Meaning it is a type of currency that is only declared legal tender by the government yet has no real intrinsic or fixed value and is not backed by any tangible asset, such as gold. Basically, our society just believes the money we use cancels our debts. Once the belief in the money is gone so is the believed value. So, is it safe to say that many of us were socially in debt before we were ever in debt financially? For example, if I had an ailment, I would seek to begin a professional relationship with a doctor due to the fact the doctor has access to resources and is knowledgeable in the field of health. People tend to seek those who complete them or fill a void. Like the old saying goes opposites attract. Look at the people you surround yourself with. Your surroundings will give you an indication of your projections. Picture a woman that always dresses provocatively. One could only imagine the personality type she attracts. My guess would be the type of individuals driven by physical needs and carnal desires. Now, let me clarify myself, I'm not saying there is anything wrong with a woman dressing sexy for a date or her husband. I'm simply pointing out one of the natural laws. There are actually seven natural laws. These are the fundamentals that govern the totality of existence.

Natural law states that human beings possess intrinsic values that govern our reasoning and behavior. They are the laws of: Attraction, Polarity, Rhythm, Relativity, Cause and Effect, Gender/Gustation and Perpetual Transmutation of Energy.

The Philosophy behind law of Attraction is that energy precedes manifestation. A flower needs to pollenate, so the pollen attracts the bees. A peacock looks to attract a suitable mate, so it displays it's beautiful feathers. The law of Polarity states that everything has an opposite, and the existence of these opposites is vital in helping us to gain a deeper understanding. The law of Rhythm states that everything is cyclical, and change is always around the corner. The law of Relativity is the law that requires challenges and failures in exchange for higher vibrations. The law of Cause-and-Effect states for every cause there is an effect. The law of Gender and Gustation states that everything in the physical universe, from concepts to matter, follows a natural process of growth and development. An example of this is sexual reproduction. The law of Perpetual Transmutation of Energy asserts that energy can neither be created nor destroyed. These are all ways nature expresses its' language in order to keep the continuation of the cycle going. Ask yourself what is your language? What is your frequency? And what do you resonate with? The answers may lie deeper than someone that you feel validates you. Through his 40 years of experience as a marriage counsellor Dr. Gary Chapman discovered there are 5 languages of love within romantic relationships, families, friendships, and leadership roles. Which are words of affirmation, receiving gifts, quality time, acts of service and physical touch.

I admire people who go out there way to refresh others. Though no one person or gender should always be on the receiving end. Some individuals have a habit of feeling entitled to being pampered.

As if, good looks, a job title, or a nice pair of breasts would cause the world to stop spinning on its axis. Be mindful of people that feel you should lay your coat at their feet continuously. Being honest with ourselves is the best policy. The truth is that some people only associate or befriend others for what they can do for them. As mature adults its important to understand the dynamics of our existence. No matter how learned a person is no one will ever have all the answers. As, long as your open to receiving the truth the universe will pour into you. Have you ever spent time with someone and felt like they really understood you? Like they could really relate to you or just knew what you were thinking. As the salt of the earth, we should be open to taking chances on people especially when they help us align with who we are called to be. Instead of placating to those who make us shrink back from our true nature. We've all heard of someone or been that someone that has refrained from doing something we love or enjoy out of fear of being reprimanded or looked down upon by someone we esteem. Embracing who we are is key to finding many answers that may be unclear. When you accept who you are in the moment you begin to understand your place in life and the people that should be in it. The circles we choose either nurture our true self or causes us to feel lost and out of place. We tend to choose friendships that add prestige to our lives rather than those that invite us to open our minds to the possibilities of who we are on the inside. Acceptance is a beautiful thing it gives the ability to see that others have a God given right to be their own distinct person, and have their own feelings, thoughts and opinions. A lot of times we select "travel buddies" to befriend.

What I mean by this is often individual refrain from unloading their emotional baggage's. It's carried from place to place. Sabotaging every relationship and friendship they may be entangled in. Life is an experience that we learn from as we live. Even though we learn from our own experiences we should also glean from those who walked before us. Our experiences teach us not to put our hands over the fire a second time. Even with experience life still purifies by fire. Fire is used as symbolism for a test. All must learn to love themselves so no one else will have to. Then when you meet that special person and true love is given it's a constellation. When we learn to love ourselves earnestly, the love, we have for ourselves make it easy for us to be ourselves. True love convicts people to grow even in the driest places. In life we must remember people grow and change. Some may grow together others grow apart. This can happen even if the love is real.

Someone you spent your entire life with could one day, wake up and feel as if they no longer know you anymore. This could be due to lack of communication and understanding where the relationship has turned. It could also be due to different worlds colliding and some of the compromises needed to keep them together eventually knocked them out of orbit. A lot of communication is directed at someone and not into the person. Time is a commodity that is never returned. So, when someone makes time for us, we should appreciate the gesture. After all some relationships fall apart due to lack of time. If you feel like you don't even have time for yourself, how will you be able to be present for someone else. Relationships are all about sacrifice. Thou sometimes partners sacrifice too much of themselves and lose their identity which leads to imbalances and possibly codependency. It's expected to lose some parts of your individuality to a degree when falling in love. Never sacrifice your total identity of who you are. Your identity is the reason your companion fell in love in the first place.

Many experiences we go through cause us to lose ourselves in the shuffle. We become like kings and queens mixed in with the rest of the other cards. We all try to learn to play the cards we're dealt hoping to get ahead in life. Ambitions have been known to turn the warm hearted cold. At the same time our quest, hopes and taste are what distinguishes us from the next. Remember seasoning can lose its flavor being left out in the cold too long. When hope is deferred it makes the heart sick. Perseverance is essential to desist from becoming bitter and vindictive. The truth is everyone will hurt you. You must choose people worth being hurt over. Often the inability to manage one's pain causes people to lash out at others normally who had nothing to do with the pain being endured.

Americans tend to feel entitled to be overwhelmed with happiness. After all, its an American right to pursuit happiness. Connections and associations I don't believe were meant to make us happy. That's something we must do for ourselves. Countless marriages have ended with the words "I'm not happy anymore". Indicating that it's the other party's responsibility to keep them happy. Instead of looking for happiness outwardly we should search for it within. We should substitute the mindset of always looking for what we can get or receive and take moments in life to seek someone we can add to in a positive way. It may seem far fetched that the very thing you're looking for in life may find its way to your doorsteps when you take on the mindset to add to another person's life. We've all heard the saying "you get out of life what you put into it". Yet have you ever put your all into something only to find yourself making no progress.

These are times it may be best to remain still because a working universe may be trying to present you with something. It's always a good idea to take a moment and step back to gain different perspectives. When you don't have the answers the wisest thing one could do would be to take time to re-evaluate the next steps before veering further off course. Its safe to say that sometimes it's our associations that's the culprit ushering us off course. Look at it this way if you planted a flower next to a weed it would be difficult for the flower to thrive. I'm not saying we should go through life thinking we are better than anyone or judging the next person. I'm simply pointing out that we feed off one another. For instance, if a person was in a rough season in their life its probably not the best idea for that person to be around someone who ignores their every word. They should be around someone who is an active listener. Communication is encoding and decoding. Some people just desire to be heard all the time which is a red flag.

Often, we hold on to what we should get off our chest because we feel it will fall upon deaf ears anyway or from fear of being vulnerable. Allowing yourself to be vulnerable with the right person gives us the mindset and understanding we don't have to always be in control producing fruits of trust. What resonates within us usually manifest around us. Meaning, Loving people will have love for you if you're a loving person. If you're a patient person people will have patience with you. If you're a peaceful person your environment will be peaceful. Likewise, if you're a joyful person you will always find joy. I've never heard of a hungry cook. This is why it's important to continuously monitor how we feel and our emotions. Its so easy to be overcome by negative thoughts and emotions especially when we feel trodden down by burdens of the world. Dealing with difficult and negative people also takes a toll on our outlook.

In the book, Dealing with Difficult People Dr. Rick Brickman and Dr. Rick Kirschner give an archetype for dealing with many different types of personalities. In their book they define the difficult personalities as follows:

The Tank: is confrontational pointed, and angry, the ultimate in pushy and aggressive behaviors.

The Sniper: uses rude comments, sarcasm, or body language to make one look odious.

The Grenade: usually delves into unfocused, ranting, and raving concerning things that have nothing to do with present circumstances.

The Know it All: is seldom in doubt, has low tolerance for correction nor contradiction. They normally are the individuals who point the finger.

The Yes Man: without thinking things thru yes people say yes to avoid confrontation. They become resentful due to being over committed and have a lack of self-time.

Procrastinator: avoids commitment for the sake of better opportunities that may arise. Most decisions have a certain window of time. They usually struggle with hopelessness.

Whiners: tend to feel overwhelmed and helpless a victim to an unfair world.

Below are excerpts of the book:

"Under normal circumstances people who are difficult to deal with tend to have a motive behind their behavior. The motive is the culprit behind behavior as well as behavior changes".

"Understanding human behavior, one should also observe an individual's level of assertiveness. Which ranges from passive to aggressive. Situations in life causes everyone to respond with a certain level of assertiveness whether they are in or out of their comfort zone. The level of assertiveness can be gauged by tone of voice, mannerism, and the content of their words".

"Some people are task focused while others are people focused. Ones conversation will generally identify if they are focused on the task or the person. Word choices tend to reflect the concern all in all a person can either be aggressive, assertive, or passive while focusing on a certain task or person."

"Peoples behavior tends to unconsciously prioritize based on what they feel is most important and their intentions whether good or bad."

The author advises their readers to remember "It's said that the road to hell is paved with those who had good intentions."

Lastly, I would like to share with my readers what the authors write "If we utilize effective communication stating clearly what our intentions are there is little to no room for misunderstanding. Beginning a relationship based off an encounter where both parties are earnest, honest, and state their true intentions mile markers and road signs are put in placed making it almost impossible to get off course. Our choice of words also helps in creating a receptive environment while building trust. Projecting what you expect when assuming the best is the best means to an end result".

"If you fall into the traps of people pleasing, you hide your true self, afraid that you will be rejected. You comprise your convictions in order to be socially acceptable and politically correct."
Rick Warren

"To gain that which is worth having, it may be necessary to lose everything else."
Countess Markievicz

Dealing with difficult people and difficult situations can be draining and stressful leaving you empty. If rejuvenation techniques and practices aren't learned a person won't have anything left to give emotionally in a relationship after dealing with normal day to day tasks. Which brings me to my next topic meditation. It's said that meditation is so powerful it can rewire our brains. Countless collegiate studies using electroencephalography and magnetic resonance imaging have shown regular meditation practices can rewrite the neural patterns in a human brain and increase grey matter as well.

To sum it up meditation leads to decreases psychological stress. Here's a list of the many health benefits of meditation.

- Gaining a new perspective on stressful situations.
- Increasing self-awareness.
- Focusing on the present.
- Reducing negative emotions.
- Increasing imagination and creativity.
- Increasing patience and tolerance.
- Improved memory
- Better focus and mental clarity
- Longer attention span.

In Psychology Today, Christopher Bergland writes, a interesting article titled: Mindfulness Meditation and the Vagus Nerve share many Powers. In the article he talks about how the stimulation of the vagus nerve and mindfulness can optimize the default mode network. He writes detailed information regarding a study that found that stimulating the vagus nerve dramatically reduces the severity of depression. He also talks about a second study dealing with mindfulness meditation that optimizes functional connectivity of the default mode network. He states it "lowered inflammation and improved the brain's ability to manage stress and anxiety". You may be wondering what is the vagus nerve and how do I stimulate it with mindful meditation? Before I go into methods of meditation let's explore the vagus nerve.

In a memoir, How to Stimulate Your Vagus Nerve for Better Mental Health Jordan Fallis describes the vagus nerve as the longest nerve in the body that connects the brain to many important organs throughout the body, including the gut, heart, and lungs. He explains that the word itself is a Latin word that means wanderer in Latin. He goes on to mention that the vagus nerve is a key part of the parasympathetic "rest and digest" nervous system and that it influences your bodies breathing, digestive function and heart rate. He quotes that "increasing your vagal tone activities the parasympathetic nervous system, and having higher vagal tone means that the body can relax faster after stress". He concludes by writing "you don't have to be controlled by your body and mind. You have the power to tell it what to do". I'm sure by now in the back of your mind you're wondering what a vagal tone is. According to NCBI vagal tone is a measure of cardiovascular function that facilitates adaptive responses to environmental challenge. Low vagal tone has been associated with poor emotional and attentional regulation and conceptualized as a marker of sensitivity to stress. Dr Arielle Schwartz comments "By developing an understanding of the workings of your vagus nerve, you may find it possible to work with your nervous system rather than feel trapped when it works against you". Practices that may stimulate the vagus nerve naturally include yoga, meditation, prayer, cold exposure, singing, fasting, and massages.

All too often we desire change but lack the capacity to create the catalyst for change. A clear mind enables us and gives us our control back. We must learn to declutter our emotional closets to create the space needed to grow. As a young sapling grows to a tree it requires more space. Its roots go deeper so it's canopy can reach higher. A lot of times we cheat ourselves due to the fact we lack the space to take in new experiences.

Normally when we no longer have space or are at capacity, we shift to survival mode. Everything feels like routine. We lower our vibration and fall lower in the taxonomic ranks behaving like mere animals. When you feel like this dark cloud is over your head break away and incorporate a new activity into your lifestyle. If you have never been to the beach, take time to get your feet wet. If you've never been skiing, take a chance and live a little even if you just use it as an excuse to seek serenity in a nice cabin at a ski resort. Life is a one-time ordeal that you will have your current identity. If we live our lives in fear, we have already lost before we began.

We also create space in our lives through forgiveness. According to Mayo Clinic "letting go of grudges and bitterness can make way for improved health and peace of mind. Forgiveness can lead to healthier relationships and improved mental health". If you've ever fallen out with a friend over money and no longer talk and still harness the grudge do yourself a favor and forgive them and release them of their debt. By doing so you will alleviate stress and allow yourself to move on. Not to mention close a door that deserves to be closed in your life. I'm not saying if they didn't repay you the first time to give them innumerable chances to take advantage of you. I am saying be mindful of patterns and know when to close certain doors. Never be too proud to walk away. Confidence looks good but humility is a virtue. Elizabeth Hardwick once stated, "Reversals and peculiarities fall down upon those too proud of their erotic life". Some people are too proud of themselves to ever think they need to revise anything. Humility is the substance that honor is made of. Too often we crave ill gotten attention and yearn to start right at the top. There are certain ethics involved in a person's dynamic that is willing and patient enough to work their way from the ground up.

When we skip steps on our way to the top, we may be prematurely putting ourselves in the forefront before we are fully developed enough to deal with what lies ahead. Maturity is the understanding that enables the determined to embrace the journey knowing we all will arrive at our destinations in the proper season. There is a divine design to everything around us. When we recognize this, we open ourselves up to countless opportunities. When we get outside the design due to impatience, we often cause ourselves agonizing disappointments in life. Life is an ominous process that gracefully distinguishes those willing to become well rounded. Mental and spiritual maturity is a process that doesn't happen overnight. I often run into successful people who seem cold, not cold hearted and detached because they desired the limelight and would do anything to get it. Bright lights aren't a bad thing as long as there are few regrets once you've become a success. Normally this is when many find out that money doesn't by happiness by then it's too late. Life requires something from us all but I would prefer not to be broken once I've made it beyond the cusp of success. Money is a tool not a mask to cover up past regrets and pain. Though shopping sprees can be quite therapeutic. Ask yourself, what is success? I'm sure your answers will vary. On the way to the top one must be mindful of people's patterns, desires, and motives. By doing so you gauge who is worthy of your time. If a person is always cutting corners and looking for the easy way-out chances are that person is an opportunist and will possibly use anything or anyone to get what they desire. Save yourself the disappointment and cut any ties. The reality is it's a cold and grim world we live in, and most people aren't worth your time. Many will do just about anything to get ahead in life. You must make an active decision that you will not compromise your integrity for your desires.

The famous scientist Charles Darwin stated "survival is not about the strong, smart, or big in stature rather those able to adapt. Ask yourself what you are willing to do to survive? What are you willing to do to become successful in your own right? Without being elusive to self, ask yourself what it is you want out of life and what it would be worth to you. Value doesn't always come in the form of a dollar sign. Knowing that some monetary gain may cause you to lose self-worth usually helps, along with some good morals and values to navigate around wolves in sheep clothing. Broken promises of fame and fortune have left thousands empty due to tangible sacrifices that return only intangible advancements. I was watching a documentary about the champion Mike Tyson. He talked about his glory days and how he was the youngest heavy weight champion. He made a profound statement that sticks with me even today. Tyson stated, "what once meant the world to me (his championship belts) now means nothing". He called his championship belts garbage compared to what he values now. Always keep in mind what you value now may change once you have lived a little and have gotten more experience under your belt. Never make a permanent decision based on a temporary situation. A sound mind is crucial in a skeptical world where so few hold to their faith in the face of adversity. If one is secure in self, he or she seldomly will cater to their id, ego, or super ego. Your personal journey for the most part is uncharted. Our journey to uncover mysteries buried deep within us take years to discover. So, it's a good rule of thumb to give yourself a little wiggle room to make mistakes. Many mentors agree that setting goals is good practice. One of the reasons being it stimulates the mind to think outside the here and now. Remember not to beat yourself up about your goals if you're not able to adhere to all of them that you set because there not set in stone. It's okay to play the game like Peyton Manning and say "Omaha" a few times to make audibles.

Everything in nature is centered around natural selection. We position ourselves in circles that improve us. The individuals closet to us have the greatest impact on our lives. When we're around those who have our best interest at heart, we feel coherent with one another. The distinct undertone of being on the same page is more than merely having an understanding. Heart brain coherency allows us to go beyond our physical limitations. Especially when we're linked with others who understand the capabilities of the mind. As we learn more about mind energy and brain waves and how they correlate to the universe, a clear understanding of who we are comes to fruition. Knowledge is continuously evolving. What was relevant yesterday is obsolete today. There is only so much water you can pour in an 8oz glass. All to often people fail to empty themselves. When you empty yourself of the old, you create space for the new. No one ask a waiter to pour more coffee into a cup already full. Even when its half full we hate being caught off guard with a refill. Runners generate more energy and endurance when they train and exhaust themselves. A runner doesn't just start out running a 10k Marathon.

Lao Tzu quoted "Watch your thoughts, they become your words; watch your words, they become your actions; watch yours actions they become your habits; watch your habits they become character; watch your character it becomes your destiny". Discipline is a crown worn by champions. Usually those who push themselves to the limit are those who set records and are remembered through the ages. Discipline is usually thought of as punishment, rarely is it ascribed as knowledge typically studied during some form of higher learning. No matter how much one studies, a person will never have all the answers, will never have the capacity to obtain all the gifts, nor receive all the human abilities.

This is why surrounding yourself with a diverse talent pool is conducive for growth and wholeness. We all excel, we just excel in different arenas. Finding and connecting with those who excel where you lack is the true meaning of 360 degrees. The circle's symbolic meaning is self, wholeness, and infinite potential. We bring harmony to our lives by understanding that in a circle all parts are equal. Life itself is full of diversity all around us whether a person is willing to accept it or not. Even though ethnic barriers still exist today, we see in marketing on tv the agenda of learning to co-exist. Logically, our understanding allows us to comprehend that all beliefs are not indoctrinated to agree with co-existence. As we journey outside our comfort zone, we stretch ourselves. For a moment, the experience may be uncomfortable or painful, but the aftermath is clear, we grow. I often hear people talk about places they've traveled to, rarely mentioning what they brought back from the journey. The lessons learned on the path to discovering one's true self are priceless souvenirs. I was listening to Td Jakes on tv he said he doesn't allow anyone who hasn't been through anything to pray for him. According to Quora research shows that people who overcome life's storms experience personal growth. Character traits like resilience, optimism, self-discipline, determination and gratitude are further developed during the process of overcoming hardships and difficulties. In agriculture, the olive and grape grow best in difficult soil. When you apply for a job, your past experience is what qualifies you for that position. Our trials and tribulations give us confidence and prepare us for the next turbulent situation. Silver must be put to the fire to be purified. The same way dross is removed from silver, our flaws are etched out. Hardships in life also expose the people around us. Successful people are normally surrounded by countless people. Hardships put relationships to the test. They allow us to see whose really for us or who is only out for gain.

You can normally look at how someone treats a person with less than they have to determine their character. Life is precious. We must be meticulous who we allow in our space. If someone is wreck less with their own life don't expect them to value yours. Our bodies are sacred temples and should be looked after as such. The physical aspect of health is just as important as the mental part. This is why exercise is essential. Our emotions are driven by brain chemicals. When a person exercises regularly the brain releases endorphins which heighten one's mood. Endorphins are peptides. They activate the body's opiate receptors causing an analgesic effect. Life is an emotional roller coaster. Those who are not grounded in a form of belief are tossed to and fro. The direction that life takes us is usually determined by how we handle the down time. Our world is governed by seasons and preparation is key to success.

"Take delight in the sun and at the sight of blooming flowers, but remember, the storms and the winter shall also surely come. Learn how to adjust your sails and know when to adjust them, prepare yourself for the cold and the stormy seasons, but remember to always enjoy the sun while it shines."

Tshepo H. Maoa

What doesn't come naturally is forced. Normally what is forced is heavily manipulated. An Armani suit given to a homeless man wouldn't change his social class if he was left on the streets. Life as he knew it would relatively remain the same. Chemistry is never about the clothes on our backs. It's about our thoughts, content of character, and nature of heart. Class is a process few go through who avidly want to differentiate themselves from others while being mindful of others. In the bible there's an ancient civilization called Babylon. Theres a story about the Nimrod era. During this time everyone spoke the same language. It's said that there was nothing impossible for them. Nimrod's society could accomplish anything their hearts desired because they had one tongue and understood power of oneness. The tongue puts in motion the decrees of the mind. Imagine if our minds came together like in the days of Babylon for a common goal. Many people have a false sense of Babylon and feel its synonymous with evil. Even in the bible it is considered the golden age of civilization. Being on one accord is a powerful phenomenon. When at least two people come together in agreement the energy present is the substance that manifest ideas. Just one person alone yelling at the top of their lungs has the magnitude to produce enough energy to power a small television. Imagine the power of 2 or 3. Genuine connections amplify our awareness and consciousness. On the flipside, connections with toxic individuals have the opposite effect.

Toxic personalities can be draining. Sometimes it's the mindset other times it due to lack of compatibility with a certain personality type. We befriend people based on certain personality traits. They may be funny, entertaining, friendly, wise, meek, earnest, honest and so forth.

Have you ever asked yourself why your drawn to certain people? How about why you attract certain people? Some believe what we harness on the inside we project on the outside, sending a reflection of us to the universe, in turn attracting our likeness. This is why intelligent people associate with smart beautiful people. Normally your environment around you is represented with in you. If you have an unclean mind more than likely your environment is also unclean. From time to time everyone should look in the mirror to evaluate themselves. If you identify with someone that never looks in the mirror, chances are their focus is outwardly and you're always under the microscope being scrutinized. Those who tend to look at themselves in the mirror often evaluate where they're at in life as far a maturity and development is concerned. Many of us discover our gifts and abilities at different stages in life. One thing is for sure its wise to remain balanced. As we honestly analyze who we've become we should also look around and accurately gauge our surroundings as well. Theres a saying "just because you knew me doesn't me you know me." Meaning people grow, metamorphize and become different figures. No one stays the same we either progress or digress. It's human nature to be fruitful. Our design is to multiply and be fruitful. Some incorporate corporations and businesses. Some cultivate churches and outreach programs. Others bring inventions into fruition. Whatever the case maybe we are all called to add to ourselves even if it's simply bringing children into the world.

Associations should be considered investments of time. So, before you invest a large portion of your time in getting to know someone be sure that your interest is beyond skin deep. Beauty is fleeting and Possessions can be lost. Looks and possessions are constellation prizes.

I, myself am guilty of investing too much time in the wrong places with the wrong people. It seems when I had a moment of clarity, I felt robbed of man's most valuable commodity, time. I said to myself "I wish I could turn back the hands of time." Then I learned to redeem my time by taking account of the full scope of my life. As we begin to see our long-lost desires and dreams being fulfilled life begins to feel more like a gift rather than a challenge. Life tends to have its way of pushing us in directions we never imagined. There are times in life where personal growth controls our direction. There are times when you'll have to operate outside your capacity of understanding. Because our knowledge doesn't go beyond our experiences and to grow, we must navigate thru uncharted territory. We live forward and understand backwards. It's funny how many of life's perplexing moments create opportunity for us to grow.

The difficult solutions sought after in life are the answers, we seek to propel us further to our destiny. Life's uncertainty can be fearful at times not knowing where to turn. It can be hard at times to make decisions based on things you hope for with evidence of things unseen. I guess that's why many have trouble grasping the concept of faith. To remain steadfast even in the crucible of humiliation takes perseverance. At times it may make us feel like grapes of wrath put to the press to be poured out as a libation. The seasons in life during these chaotic moments when we feel like all hell is breaking loose our ingredients are revealed. Trying times show us what we're made of. It's easy to be in a parade when the forecast is sunshine. Accurate accounts of our lives are mile markers. It's said that one putting on his armor shouldn't boast like one taking off his armor. It's a constant war going on in our minds. We must continuously win the battle in our minds before we can be victorious elsewhere.

Lost wisdom is like hidden treasure it has no value till found. When we find the lost treasure buried deep within us our self-worth becomes clear. How can you know your self-worth if you fail to realize your innate abilities and gifts? Deep within every human being there's a cognitive ability designed for greatness. An educated and enlightened society is a well-informed thriving republic. The absence of knowledge is the beginning of perils. When intelligence, harmony, and productivity are in accord true democracy is born. As we educate ourselves one becomes enlightened pushing back corruption. A corrupt mind is a corrupt body. No matter if it's on the left or the right of the bicameral governing body, corruption pervades throughout. It's the same with individuals on a personal level. Our actions, decisions, and thoughts are what govern us and those around us. Circle of associations can be broken down into three groups. Those who identify with a cause. Those who support you and those who share a common foe or problem. Yokes begin to be broken when you're aligned with those assigned to your purpose. Wise words spoken over your life can be liberating. A person's heart tends to reveal their situation. It's written that the heart can reveal your situation better than seven sentinels on a tower.

A pure heart and sound mind are virtuous delicacies that few have the honor to indulge in. The wiles of the world pollute the thoughts and desires of many. As the "world" manufactures ill-gotten gain the impure billows of smoke pervade our lives blinding many from finding their path. The inability to inhale life's purest gifts inhibits us from exhaling the enjoyment of life's perfect peace. The lens of appreciation should always be placed on our blessings. There is always something to be thankful for.

The learned grow to become more understanding of the weights placed on the scale of life to find balance without compromising integrity and virtues. The fabrics of this world are woven together by the gifts humanity has given. Like a tree that branches out to provide shade, our fruits and labor also provide shelter for those fortunate enough to partake. Good fortune happens when we align with good energy. Even in the bible it talks about virtue going out from Yeshua. This is the mystical part about life you never know who you could be entertaining when talking to strangers. We are 11-dimensional beings in a 3-dimensional experience. This is how seers, Prophets, and psychics see beyond the present. I don't want to delve too deep into this topic. It's just a bullet point to explain we must extend our experiences beyond our sight and perspectives. We are spiritual beings first. Even though our design is fashioned based on our experiences and those around us. There is also a divine design for every one of us. The more time we spend with ourselves we awaken new possibilities. Individuals who understand universal laws carry a trait allowing them to speak a thought into manifestation. The universe has a pernicious way of being affectionate with those who are accustomed to being aware of their atmosphere. When we're in tuned to the world around us our mind reaches out beyond the present. The universe protects those who hold majestic secrets. The world as we know it is changing all around us. Our ability to invoke adaptation is a must to a certain degree. This is why it is important to surround yourself with infallible individuals who possess a valiant sense of esteem and virtue. Most people tend to view the mind as intellect, volition, and feelings. Rarely do we perceive the mind as a group conjoined by qualities and virtues. No one truly knows to what extent our minds interact with one another. Life is a perennial process. Those unaware of the different seasons in life usually leave us drained and out of sync.

When everyone around us is in sync the ability to produce a desired outcome is phenomenal. Problems tend to arise when our counterparts are not on the same page. The conglomerate is left out of balance. Wise counsel is key to success. Rarely are plans abated when they are constructed by individuals who are knowledgeable in that field. If we possess active mental strength, it's only natural for others to be drawn to us. Be aware that this is the same reason the rose bloom is cut and placed in a vase. The moves we make bring the show to fruition. The words we speak sell the tickets. Human admiration is natural. This is why boundaries are important. Learn to surround yourself with those who have the same appetite for truth. If you're the smartest one in the room, it's often said you're in the wrong room. When we stimulate our minds the dimensions of our thoughts change. They begin to square the circle. The sovereign hopes of the just shall avail many within a circle. In reality, there will always be a judas. Some will always fall by the wayside. Many who lack balance in life will always look to attach to those in harmony. Acquisitive desires push our ever-evolving society to a brink where men step on one another beyond reason. Within our quest to obtain our desires know that there is always a median between extremes. If the mind truly has the ability to communicate through extrasensory perception, the ability itself alleviates many possibilities of personal boundaries. Picture a group of intellectuals coming together as one body or what I call an Impetus mind. Every goal and task would be cemented by an unalloyed force. Driving a selflessness agenda. Self-centered individuals in power tend to sow discord leading to the separation of society into small groups for wrong reasons. As we learn more about communication and the importance of linguistics we begin to understand the significance of controlled arguments. No matter how many similarities we share there will always be opposite views.

How we handle our disagreements display our level of maturity. Felicitous colleagues and companions covey a substratum truth about ourselves. Anything worth being in your life should be tried by a litmus test. We must learn to be patient in our practical affairs as we discover ourselves. The more we learn about ourselves ensure that we're not forcing puzzle pieces to fit. Throughout life everyone of us will come into contact with a large volume of people similar to a great body of water. It's our responsibility to filter through those who are stagnant. When we are balanced we find ourselves around well-rounded people. "Equilibrium" occurs when one is mindful of each other's morals, our own integrity, health, and immaterial essence. If we spend all our time dealing with religion one becomes to pious. Like wise if we spend all our time increasing our physicality we put all our trust in our own strength. Both attributes are great qualities. It's just focusing solely on one aspect of life causes us to miss out on others. As we are drawn to and select those around us remember those who remain understanding and connected with us even when our presence is no longer a novelty are those usually connected to our calling. As we learn to identify what drives us we begin to unyoke with those who lack our identifiers. What we feed our minds is what we become. If you give a man books pertaining to business he will become a businessman. If you give a man books containing laws and statues he will become a lawyer. What we digest is what we become as well as the circles we find ourselves in. Those who we seek out to invest our time with are normally headed in our same direction. You don't hop on a plane headed to London if your destination is New York. Never allow your life's progress to be impeded for simple gratification or temporary pleasures. When someone's main agenda is self their communication speaks volume but their actions are minimal.

As we navigate through life's labyrinth we must get accustom to walking some roads alone. During the journey, in the knowing is where our awareness grows allowing us to matriculate into impetus minds. When we become dissolved into impetus minds we embody something larger than ourselves reflecting our unison with in the fields that we all co-exist.

"All evidence available in the biological sciences support the core proposition... That the cosmos is a specially designed whole in which all facets of reality have their meaning and explanation in this central fact"
Dr. Michael Denton

Designers Price

If I never knew my worth I'd be willing to accept anything that came along the way.

If I didn't know who I was it's a certainty that there would be people willing to tell me.

If I didn't define myself someone else would define me by definition.

If I didn't distinguish myself I would fit in in just about any setting.

Instead of dissolving into just any elements around, precious things maintain their identity. Webster defines the word dissolving as to separate into component parts. To waste or fade away. To be overcome emotionally. Life's convoluted course, at times is very overwhelming. We become overly absorbed in our emotions. Eventually breaking ourselves down to only have to pick up the pieces. The intricate thing about life is no one's design is identical. So even if you have a prolific mentor in your life. You should keep in mind that no matter how many similarities the two of you have the design will always be unique. The model of everyone's life is conceived to bring about an intended end. We all have a specific design, and function. When we discover the design for our lives, life's beneficial effects begin to manifest fruitfully all of our days.

Excerpts from "Desire of the Ages"

"It is not the highest work of education to communicate knowledge merely, but to import that vitalizing energy which is received through the contact of mind with mind and soul with soul."

"The measure of divine attention bestowed on any object is proportionate to its rank in scale of being."

"Words are an indication of that which is in the heart, but words are more than an indication of character; they have power to react on the character."

"Inspiration stoops to give no reason. An unseen presence, it speaks to mind and soul, and moves the heart to action. It is its own justification."

"It's the sails not the gales that determine where we shall go. We set our sails and choose our path in faith using the winds of adversity to our advantage."

"We will reap what we sow; the eternal harvest is equal to the planting in our mental activity."

Words of Wisdom

- A true social morality will ensure prosperity.
- No man can be true to principle without exciting opposition.
- The perception and appreciation of truth depends less upon the mind than upon the heart.
- When planning for a year plant corn. When planning for a decade plant trees. When planning for a life train people.
- "The tunnel of conflict is the passage way to intimacy". **Rick Warren**
- Most conflict Is rooted in unmet needs.
- "The soul never thinks without a picture." **Aristotle**
- "Research has shown that one's thought life influences every aspect of ones being." **Archibald Hart**
- "Pain nourishes courage. You can't be brave if you've only had wonderful things happen to you" **Mary Tyler Moore**

Hammurabi's Code

1. If any one ensnare another, putting a ban upon him, but he can not prove it, then he that ensnared him shall be put to death.

2. If any one bring an accusation against a man, and the accused go to the river and leap into the river, if he sink in the river his accuser shall take possession of his house. But if the river prove that the accused is not guilty, and he escape unhurt, then he who had brought the accusation shall be put to death, while he who leaped into the river shall take possession of the house that had belonged to his accuser.

3. If any one bring an accusation of any crime before the elders, and does not prove what he has charged, he shall, if it be a capital offense charged, be put to death.

4. If he satisfy the elders to impose a fine of grain or money, he shall receive the fine that the action produces.

5. If a judge try a case, reach a decision, and present his judgment in writing; if later error shall appear in his decision, and it be through his own fault, then he shall pay twelve times the fine set by him in the case, and he shall be publicly removed from

the judge's bench, and never again shall he sit there to render judgement.

6. 7If any one steal the property of a temple or of the court, he shall be put to death, and also the one who receives the stolen thing from him shall be put to death.

7. If any one buy from the son or the slave of another man, without witnesses or a contract, silver or gold, a male or female slave, an ox or a sheep, an ass or anything, or if he take it in charge, he is considered a thief and shall be put to death.

8. If any one steal cattle or sheep, or an ass, or a pig or a goat, if it belong to a god or to the court, the thief shall pay thirtyfold therefor; if they belonged to a freed man of the king he shall pay tenfold; if the thief has nothing with which to pay he shall be put to death.

9. If any one lose an article, and find it in the possession of another: if the person in whose possession the thing is found say "A merchant sold it to me, I paid for it before witnesses," and if the owner of the thing say, "I will bring witnesses who know my property," then shall the purchaser bring the merchant who sold it to him, and the witnesses before whom he bought it, and the owner shall bring witnesses who can identify his property. The judge shall examine their testimony--both of the witnesses before whom the price was paid, and of the witnesses who identify the lost article on oath. The merchant is then proved to be a thief and shall be put to death.

The owner of the lost article receives his property, and he who bought it receives the money he paid from the estate of the merchant.

10. If the purchaser does not bring the merchant and the witnesses before whom he bought the article, but its owner bring witnesses who identify it, then the buyer is the thief and shall be put to death, and the owner receives the lost article.

11. If the owner do not bring witnesses to identify the lost article, he is an evil-doer, he has traduced, and shall be put to death.

12. If the witnesses be not at hand, then shall the judge set a limit, at the expiration of six months. If his witnesses have not appeared within the six months, he is an evil-doer, and shall bear the fine of the pending case.

13. If any one steal the minor son of another, he shall be put to death.

14. If any one take a male or female slave of the court, or a male or female slave of a freed man, outside the city gates, he shall be put to death.

15. If any one receive into his house a runaway male or female slave of the court, or of a freedman, and does not bring it out at the public proclamation of the major domus, the master of the house shall be put to death.

16. If any one find runaway male or female slaves in the open country and bring them to their masters, the master of the slaves shall pay him two shekels of silver.

17. If the slave will not give the name of the master, the finder shall bring him to the palace; a further investigation must follow, and the slave shall be returned to his master.

18. If he hold the slaves in his house, and they are caught there, he shall be put to death.

19. If the slave that he caught run away from him, then shall he swear to the owners of the slave, and he is free of all blame.

20. If any one break a hole into a house (break in to steal), he shall be put to death before that hole and be buried.

21. If any one is committing a robbery and is caught, then he shall be put to death.

22. If the robber is not caught, then shall he who was robbed claim under oath the amount of his loss; then shall the community, and . . . on whose ground and territory and in whose domain it was compensate him for the goods stolen.

23. If persons are stolen, then shall the community and . . . pay one mina of silver to their relatives.

24. If fire break out in a house, and some one who comes to put it out cast his eye upon the property of the owner of the house, and take the property of the master of the house, he shall be thrown into that self-same fire.

25. If a chieftain or a man (common soldier), who has been ordered to go upon the king's highway for war does not go, but hires a mercenary, if he withholds the compensation, then shall this

officer or man be put to death, and he who represented him shall take possession of his house.

26. If a chieftain or man be caught in the misfortune of the king (captured in battle), and if his fields and garden be given to another and he take possession, if he return and reaches his place, his field and garden shall be returned to him, he shall take it over again.

27. If a chieftain or a man be caught in the misfortune of a king, if his son is able to enter into possession, then the field and garden shall be given to him, he shall take over the fee of his father.

28. If his son is still young, and can not take possession, a third of the field and garden shall be given to his mother, and she shall bring him up.

29. If a chieftain or a man leave his house, garden, and field and hires it out, and some one else takes possession of his house, garden, and field and uses it for three years: if the first owner return and claims his house, garden, and field, it shall not be given to him, but he who has taken possession of it and used it shall continue to use it.

30. If he hire it out for one year and then return, the house, garden, and field shall be given back to him, and he shall take it over again.

31. If a chieftain or a man is captured on the "Way of the King" (in war), and a merchant buy him free, and bring him back

to his place; if he have the means in his house to buy his freedom, he shall buy himself free: if he have nothing in his house with which to buy himself free, he shall be bought free by the temple of his community; if there be nothing in the temple with which to buy him free, the court shall buy his freedom. His field, garden, and house shall not be given for the purchase of his freedom.

32. If a . . . or a . . . enter himself as withdrawn from the "Way of the King," and send a mercenary as substitute, but withdraw him, then the . . . or . . . shall be put to death.

33. If a . . . or a . . . harm the property of a captain, injure the captain, or take away from the captain a gift presented to him by the king, then the . . . or . . . shall be put to death.

34. If any one buy the cattle or sheep which the king has given to chieftains from him, he loses his money.

35. The field, garden, and house of a chieftain, of a man, or of one subject to quit-rent, can not be sold.

36. If any one buy the field, garden, and house of a chieftain, man, or one subject to quit-rent, his contract tablet of sale shall be broken (declared invalid) and he loses his money. The field, garden, and house return to their owners.

37. A chieftain, man, or one subject to quit-rent can not assign his tenure of field, house, and garden to his wife or daughter, nor can he assign it for a debt.

38. He may, however, assign a field, garden, or house which he has bought, and holds as property, to his wife or daughter or give it for debt.

39. He may sell field, garden, and house to a merchant (royal agents) or to any other public official, the buyer holding field, house, and garden for its usufruct.

40. If any one fence in the field, garden, and house of a chieftain, man, or one subject to quit-rent, furnishing the palings therefor; if the chieftain, man, or one subject to quit-rent return to field, garden, and house, the palings which were given to him become his property.

41. If any one take over a field to till it, and obtain no harvest therefrom, it must be proved that he did no work on the field, and he must deliver grain, just as his neighbor raised, to the owner of the field.

42. If he do not till the field, but let it lie fallow, he shall give grain like his neighbor's to the owner of the field, and the field which he let lie fallow he must plow and sow and return to its owner.

43. If any one take over a waste-lying field to make it arable, but is lazy, and does not make it arable, he shall plow the fallow field in the fourth year, harrow it and till it, and give it back to its owner, and for each ten gan (a measure of area) ten gur of grain shall be paid.

44. If a man rent his field for tillage for a fixed rental, and receive the rent of his field, but bad weather come and destroy the harvest, the injury falls upon the tiller of the soil.

45. If he do not receive a fixed rental for his field, but lets it on half or third shares of the harvest, the grain on the field shall be divided proportionately between the tiller and the owner.

46. If the tiller, because he did not succeed in the first year, has had the soil tilled by others, the owner may raise no objection; the field has been cultivated and he receives the harvest according to agreement.

47. If any one owe a debt for a loan, and a storm prostrates the grain, or the harvest fail, or the grain does not grow for lack of water; in that year he need not give his creditor any grain, he washes his debt-tablet in water and pays no rent for this year.

48. If any one take money from a merchant, and give the merchant a field tillable for corn or sesame and order him to plant corn or sesame in the field, and to harvest the crop; if the cultivator plant corn or sesame in the field, at the harvest the corn or sesame that is in the field shall belong to the owner of the field and he shall pay corn as rent, for the money he received from the merchant, and the livelihood of the cultivator shall he give to the merchant.

49. If he give a cultivated corn-field or a cultivated sesame-field, the corn or sesame in the field shall belong to the owner of the field, and he shall return the money to the merchant as rent.

50. If he have no money to repay, then he shall pay in corn or sesame in place of the money as rent for what he received from the merchant, according to the royal tariff.

51. If the cultivator do not plant corn or sesame in the field, the debtor's contract is not weakened.

52. If any one be too lazy to keep his dam in proper condition, and does not so keep it; if then the dam break and all the fields be flooded, then shall he in whose dam the break occurred be sold for money, and the money shall replace the corn which he has caused to be ruined.

53. If he be not able to replace the corn, then he and his possessions shall be divided among the farmers whose corn he has flooded.

54. If any one open his ditches to water his crop, but is careless, and the water flood the field of his neighbor, then he shall pay his neighbor corn for his loss.

55. If a man let in the water, and the water overflow the plantation of his neighbor, he shall pay ten gur of corn for every ten gan of land.

56. If a shepherd, without the permission of the owner of the field, and without the knowledge of the owner of the sheep, lets the sheep into a field to graze, then the owner of the field shall harvest his crop, and the shepherd, who had pastured his flock there without permission of the owner of the field, shall pay to the owner twenty gur of corn for every ten gan.

57. If after the flocks have left the pasture and been shut up in the common fold at the city gate, any shepherd let them into a field and they graze there, this shepherd shall take possession of the field which he has allowed to be grazed on, and at the harvest he must pay sixty gur of corn for every ten gan.

58. If any man, without the knowledge of the owner of a garden, fell a tree in a garden he shall pay half a mina in money.

59. If any one give over a field to a gardener, for him to plant it as a garden, if he work at it, and care for it for four years, in the fifth year the owner and the gardener shall divide it, the owner taking his part in charge.

60. If the gardener has not completed the planting of the field, leaving one part unused, this shall be assigned to him as his.

61. If he do not plant the field that was given over to him as a garden, if it be arable land (for corn or sesame) the gardener shall pay the owner the produce of the field for the years that he let it lie fallow, according to the product of neighboring fields, put the field in arable condition and return it to its owner.

62. If he transform waste land into arable fields and return it to its owner, the latter shall pay him for one year ten gur for ten gan.

63. If any one hand over his garden to a gardener to work, the gardener shall pay to its owner two-thirds of the produce of the garden, for so long as he has it in possession, and the other third shall he keep.

64. If the gardener do not work in the garden and the product fall off, the gardener shall pay in proportion to other neighboring gardens. [Here a portion of the text is missing, apparently comprising thirty-four paragraphs.]

65. Interest for the money, as much as he has received, he shall give a note therefor, and on the day, when they settle, pay to the merchant.

66. If there are no mercantile arrangements in the place whither he went, he shall leave the entire amount of money which he received with the broker to give to the merchant.

67. If a merchant entrust money to an agent (broker) for some investment, and the broker suffer a loss in the place to which he goes, he shall make good the capital to the merchant.

68. If, while on the journey, an enemy take away from him anything that he had, the broker shall swear by God and be free of obligation.

69. If a merchant give an agent corn, wool, oil, or any other goods to transport, the agent shall give a receipt for the amount, and compensate the merchant therefor. Then he shall obtain a receipt form the merchant for the money that he gives the merchant.

70. If the agent is careless, and does not take a receipt for the money which he gave the merchant, he can not consider the unreceipted money as his own.

71. If the agent accept money from the merchant, but have a quarrel with the merchant (denying the receipt), then shall the merchant swear before God and witnesses that he has given this money to the agent, and the agent shall pay him three times the sum.

72. If the merchant cheat the agent, in that as the latter has returned to him all that had been given him, but the merchant denies the receipt of what had been returned to him, then shall this agent convict the merchant before God and the judges, and if he still deny receiving what the agent had given him shall pay six times the sum to the agent.

73. If a tavern-keeper (feminine) does not accept corn according to gross weight in payment of drink, but takes money, and the price of the drink is less than that of the corn, she shall be convicted and thrown into the water.

74. If conspirators meet in the house of a tavern-keeper, and these conspirators are not captured and delivered to the court, the tavern-keeper shall be put to death.

75. If a "sister of a god" open a tavern, or enter a tavern to drink, then shall this woman be burned to death.

76. If an inn-keeper furnish sixty ka of usakani-drink to . . . she shall receive fifty ka of corn at the harvest.

77. If any one be on a journey and entrust silver, gold, precious stones, or any movable property to another, and wish to recover it from him; if the latter do not bring all of the property to

the appointed place, but appropriate it to his own use, then shall this man, who did not bring the property to hand it over, be convicted, and he shall pay fivefold for all that had been entrusted to him.

78. If any one have consignment of corn or money, and he take from the granary or box without the knowledge of the owner, then shall he who took corn without the knowledge of the owner out of the granary or money out of the box be legally convicted, and repay the corn he has taken. And he shall lose whatever commission was paid to him, or due him.

79. If a man have no claim on another for corn and money, and try to demand it by force, he shall pay one-third of a mina of silver in every case.

80. If any one have a claim for corn or money upon another and imprison him; if the prisoner die in prison a natural death, the case shall go no further.

81. If the prisoner die in prison from blows or maltreatment, the master of the prisoner shall convict the merchant before the judge. If he was a free-born man, the son of the merchant shall be put to death; if it was a slave, he shall pay one-third of a mina of gold, and all that the master of the prisoner gave he shall forfeit.

82. If any one fail to meet a claim for debt, and sell himself, his wife, his son, and daughter for money or give them away to forced labor: they shall work for three years in the house of

the man who bought them, or the proprietor, and in the fourth year they shall be set free.

83. If he give a male or female slave away for forced labor, and the merchant sublease them, or sell them for money, no objection can be raised.

84. If any one fail to meet a claim for debt, and he sell the maid servant who has borne him children, for money, the money which the merchant has paid shall be repaid to him by the owner of the slave and she shall be freed.

85. If any one store corn for safe keeping in another person's house, and any harm happen to the corn in storage, or if the owner of the house open the granary and take some of the corn, or if especially he deny that the corn was stored in his house: then the owner of the corn shall claim his corn before God (on oath), and the owner of the house shall pay its owner for all of the corn that he took.

86. If any one store corn in another man's house he shall pay him storage at the rate of one gur for every five ka of corn per year.

87. If any one give another silver, gold, or anything else to keep, he shall show everything to some witness, draw up a contract, and then hand it over for safe keeping.

88. If he turn it over for safe keeping without witness or contract, and if he to whom it was given deny it, then he has no legitimate claim.

89. If any one deliver silver, gold, or anything else to another for safe keeping, before a witness, but he deny it, he shall be brought before a judge, and all that he has denied he shall pay in full.

90. If any one place his property with another for safe keeping, and there, either through thieves or robbers, his property and the property of the other man be lost, the owner of the house, through whose neglect the loss took place, shall compensate the owner for all that was given to him in charge. But the owner of the house shall try to follow up and recover his property, and take it away from the thief.

91. If any one who has not lost his goods state that they have been lost, and make false claims: if he claim his goods and amount of injury before God, even though he has not lost them, he shall be fully compensated for all his loss claimed. (I.e., the oath is all that is needed.)

92. If any one "point the finger" (slander) at a sister of a god or the wife of any one, and can not prove it, this man shall be taken before the judges and his brow shall be marked. (by cutting the skin, or perhaps hair.)

93. If a man take a woman to wife, but have no intercourse with her, this woman is no wife to him.

94. If a man's wife be surprised (in flagrante delicto) with another man, both shall be tied and thrown into the water, but the husband may pardon his wife and the king his slaves.

95. If a man violate the wife (betrothed or child-wife) of another man, who has never known a man, and still lives in her father's house, and sleep with her and be surprised, this man shall be put to death, but the wife is blameless.

96. If a man bring a charge against one's wife, but she is not surprised with another man, she must take an oath and then may return to her house.

97. If the "finger is pointed" at a man's wife about another man, but she is not caught sleeping with the other man, she shall jump into the river for her husband.

98. If a man is taken prisoner in war, and there is a sustenance in his house, but his wife leave house and court, and go to another house: because this wife did not keep her court, and went to another house, she shall be judicially condemned and thrown into the water.

99. If any one be captured in war and there is not sustenance in his house, if then his wife go to another house this woman shall be held blameless.

100. If a man be taken prisoner in war and there be no sustenance in his house and his wife go to another house and bear children; and if later her husband return and come to his home: then this wife shall return to her husband, but the children follow their father.

101. If any one leave his house, run away, and then his wife go to another house, if then he return, and wishes to take his wife

back: because he fled from his home and ran away, the wife of this runaway shall not return to her husband.

102. If a man wish to separate from a woman who has borne him children, or from his wife who has borne him children: then he shall give that wife her dowry, and a part of the usufruct of field, garden, and property, so that she can rear her children. When she has brought up her children, a portion of all that is given to the children, equal as that of one son, shall be given to her. She may then marry the man of her heart.

103. If a man wishes to separate from his wife who has borne him no children, he shall give her the amount of her purchase money and the dowry which she brought from her father's house, and let her go.

104. If there was no purchase price he shall give her one mina of gold as a gift of release.

105. If he be a freed man he shall give her one-third of a mina of gold.

106. If a man's wife, who lives in his house, wishes to leave it, plunges into debt, tries to ruin her house, neglects her husband, and is judicially convicted: if her husband offer her release, she may go on her way, and he gives her nothing as a gift of release. If her husband does not wish to release her, and if he take another wife, she shall remain as servant in her husband's house.

107. If a woman quarrel with her husband, and say: "You are not congenial to me," the reasons for her prejudice must be presented. If she is guiltless, and there is no fault on her part, but he leaves and neglects her, then no guilt attaches to this woman, she shall take her dowry and go back to her father's house.

108. If she is not innocent, but leaves her husband, and ruins her house, neglecting her husband, this woman shall be cast into the water.

109. If a man take a wife and this woman give her husband a maid-servant, and she bear him children, but this man wishes to take another wife, this shall not be permitted to him; he shall not take a second wife.

110. If a man take a wife, and she bear him no children, and he intend to take another wife: if he take this second wife, and bring her into the house, this second wife shall not be allowed equality with his wife.

111. If a man take a wife and she give this man a maid-servant as wife and she bear him children, and then this maid assume equality with the wife: because she has borne him children her master shall not sell her for money, but he may keep her as a slave, reckoning her among the maid-servants.

112. If she have not borne him children, then her mistress may sell her for money.

113. If a man take a wife, and she be seized by disease, if he then desire to take a second wife he shall not put away his wife, who has been attacked by disease, but he shall keep her in the house which he has built and support her so long as she lives.

114. If this woman does not wish to remain in her husband's house, then he shall compensate her for the dowry that she brought with her from her father's house, and she may go.

115. If a man give his wife a field, garden, and house and a deed therefor, if then after the death of her husband the sons raise no claim, then the mother may bequeath all to one of her sons whom she prefers, and need leave nothing to his brothers.

116. If a woman who lived in a man's house made an agreement with her husband, that no creditor can arrest her, and has given a document therefor: if that man, before he married that woman, had a debt, the creditor can not hold the woman for it. But if the woman, before she entered the man's house, had contracted a debt, her creditor can not arrest her husband therefor.

117. If after the woman had entered the man's house, both contracted a debt, both must pay the merchant.

118. If the wife of one man on account of another man has their mates (her husband and the other man's wife) murdered, both of them shall be impaled.

119. If a man be guilty of incest with his daughter, he shall be driven from the place (exiled).

120. If a man betroth a girl to his son, and his son have intercourse with her, but he (the father) afterward defile her, and be surprised, then he shall be bound and cast into the water (drowned).

121. If a man betroth a girl to his son, but his son has not known her, and if then he defile her, he shall pay her half a gold mina, and compensate her for all that she brought out of her father's house. She may marry the man of her heart.

122. If any one be guilty of incest with his mother after his father, both shall be burned.

123. If any one be surprised after his father with his chief wife, who has borne children, he shall be driven out of his father's house.

124. If any one, who has brought chattels into his father-in-law's house, and has paid the purchase-money, looks for another wife, and says to his father-in-law: "I do not want your daughter," the girl's father may keep all that he had brought.

125. If a man bring chattels into the house of his father-in-law, and pay the "purchase price" (for his wife): if then the father of the girl say: "I will not give you my daughter," he shall give him back all that he brought with him.

126. If a man bring chattels into his father-in-law's house and pay the "purchase price," if then his friend slander him, and his father-in-law say to the young husband: "You shall not marry my daughter," the he shall give back to him undiminished all

that he had brought with him; but his wife shall not be married to the friend.

127. If a man marry a woman, and she bear sons to him; if then this woman die, then shall her father have no claim on her dowry; this belongs to her sons.

128. If a man marry a woman and she bear him no sons; if then this woman die, if the "purchase price" which he had paid into the house of his father-in-law is repaid to him, her husband shall have no claim upon the dowry of this woman; it belongs to her father's house.

129. If his father-in-law do not pay back to him the amount of the "purchase price" he may subtract the amount of the "Purchase price" from the dowry, and then pay the remainder to her father's house.

130. If a man give to one of his sons whom he prefers a field, garden, and house, and a deed therefor: if later the father die, and the brothers divide the estate, then they shall first give him the present of his father, and he shall accept it; and the rest of the paternal property shall they divide.

131. If a man take wives for his son, but take no wife for his minor son, and if then he die: if the sons divide the estate, they shall set aside besides his portion the money for the "purchase price" for the minor brother who had taken no wife as yet, and secure a wife for him.

132. If a man marry a wife and she bear him children: if this wife die and he then take another wife and she bear him children: if then the father die, the sons must not partition the estate according to the mothers, they shall divide the dowries of their mothers only in this way; the paternal estate they shall divide equally with one another.

133. If a man wish to put his son out of his house, and declare before the judge: "I want to put my son out," then the judge shall examine into his reasons. If the son be guilty of no great fault, for which he can be rightfully put out, the father shall not put him out.

134. If he be guilty of a grave fault, which should rightfully deprive him of the filial relationship, the father shall forgive him the first time; but if he be guilty of a grave fault a second time the father may deprive his son of all filial relation.

135. If his wife bear sons to a man, or his maid-servant have borne sons, and the father while still living says to the children whom his maid-servant has borne: "My sons," and he count them with the sons of his wife; if then the father die, then the sons of the wife and of the maid-servant shall divide the paternal property in common. The son of the wife is to partition and choose.

136. If, however, the father while still living did not say to the sons of the maid-servant: "My sons," and then the father dies, then the sons of the maid-servant shall not share with the sons of

the wife, but the freedom of the maid and her sons shall be granted. The sons of the wife shall have no right to enslave the sons of the maid; the wife shall take her dowry (from her father), and the gift that her husband gave her and deeded to her (separate from dowry, or the purchase-money paid her father), and live in the home of her husband: so long as she lives she shall use it, it shall not be sold for money. Whatever she leaves shall belong to her children.

137. If her husband made her no gift, she shall be compensated for her gift, and she shall receive a portion from the estate of her husband, equal to that of one child. If her sons oppress her, to force her out of the house, the judge shall examine into the matter, and if the sons are at fault the woman shall not leave her husband's house. If the woman desire to leave the house, she must leave to her sons the gift which her husband gave her, but she may take the dowry of her father's house. Then she may marry the man of her heart.

138. If this woman bear sons to her second husband, in the place to which she went, and then die, her earlier and later sons shall divide the dowry between them.

139. If she bear no sons to her second husband, the sons of her first husband shall have the dowry.

140. If a State slave or the slave of a freed man marry the daughter of a free man, and children are born, the master of the slave shall have no right to enslave the children of the free.

141. If, however, a State slave or the slave of a freed man marry a man's daughter, and after he marries her she bring a dowry from a father's house, if then they both enjoy it and found a household, and accumulate means, if then the slave die, then she who was free born may take her dowry, and all that her husband and she had earned; she shall divide them into two parts, one-half the master for the slave shall take, and the other half shall the free-born woman take for her children. If the free-born woman had no gift she shall take all that her husband and she had earned and divide it into two parts; and the master of the slave shall take one-half and she shall take the other for her children.

142. If a widow, whose children are not grown, wishes to enter another house (remarry), she shall not enter it without the knowledge of the judge. If she enter another house the judge shall examine the state of the house of her first husband. Then the house of her first husband shall be entrusted to the second husband and the woman herself as managers. And a record must be made thereof. She shall keep the house in order, bring up the children, and not sell the house-hold utensils. He who buys the utensils of the children of a widow shall lose his money, and the goods shall return to their owners.

143. If a "devoted woman" or a prostitute to whom her father has given a dowry and a deed therefor, but if in this deed it is not stated that she may bequeath it as she pleases, and has not

explicitly stated that she has the right of disposal; if then her father die, then her brothers shall hold her field and garden, and give her corn, oil, and milk according to her portion, and satisfy her. If her brothers do not give her corn, oil, and milk according to her share, then her field and garden shall support her. She shall have the usufruct of field and garden and all that her father gave her so long as she lives, but she can not sell or assign it to others. Her position of inheritance belongs to her brothers.

144. If a "sister of a god," or a prostitute, receive a gift from her father, and a deed in which it has been explicitly stated that she may dispose of it as she pleases, and give her complete disposition thereof: if then her father die, then she may leave her property to whomsoever she pleases. Her brothers can raise no claim thereto.

145. If a father give a present to his daughter--either marriageable or a prostitute unmarriageable)--and then die, then she is to receive a portion as a child from the paternal estate, and enjoy its usufruct so long as she lives. Her estate belongs to her brothers.

146. If a father devote a temple-maid or temple-virgin to God and give her no present: if then the father die, she shall receive the third of a child's portion from the inheritance of her father's house, and enjoy its usufruct so long as she lives. Her estate belongs to her brothers.

147. If a father devote his daughter as a wife of Mardi of Babylon (as in 181), and give her no present, nor a deed; if then her father die, then shall she receive one-third of her portion as a child of her father's house from her brothers, but Marduk may leave her estate to whomsoever she wishes.

148. If a man give his daughter by a concubine a dowry, and a husband, and a deed; if then her father die, she shall receive no portion from the paternal estate.

149. If a man do not give a dowry to his daughter by a concubine, and no husband; if then her father die, her brother shall give her a dowry according to her father's wealth and secure a husband for her.

150. If a man adopt a child and to his name as son, and rear him, this grown son can not be demanded back again.

151. If a man adopt a son, and if after he has taken him he injure his foster father and mother, then this adopted son shall return to his father's house.

152. The son of a paramour in the palace service, or of a prostitute, can not be demanded back.

153. If an artizan has undertaken to rear a child and teaches him his craft, he can not be demanded back.

154. If he has not taught him his craft, this adopted son may return to his father's house.

155. If a man does not maintain a child that he has adopted as a son and reared with his other children, then his adopted son may return to his father's house.

156. If a man, who had adopted a son and reared him, founded a household, and had children, wish to put this adopted son out, then this son shall not simply go his way. His adoptive father shall give him of his wealth one-third of a child's portion, and then he may go. He shall not give him of the field, garden, and house.

157. If a son of a paramour or a prostitute say to his adoptive father or mother: "You are not my father, or my mother," his tongue shall be cut off.

158. If the son of a paramour or a prostitute desire his father's house, and desert his adoptive father and adoptive mother, and goes to his father's house, then shall his eye be put out.

159. If a man give his child to a nurse and the child die in her hands, but the nurse unbeknown to the father and mother nurse another child, then they shall convict her of having nursed another child without the knowledge of the father and mother and her breasts shall be cut off.

160. If a son strike his father, his hands shall be hewn off.

161. If a man put out the eye of another man, his eye shall be put out. [An eye for an eye]

162. If he break another man's bone, his bone shall be broken.

163. If he put out the eye of a freed man, or break the bone of a freed man, he shall pay one gold mina.

164. If he put out the eye of a man's slave, or break the bone of a man's slave, he shall pay one-half of its value.

165. If a man knock out the teeth of his equal, his teeth shall be knocked out. [A tooth for a tooth]

166. If he knock out the teeth of a freed man, he shall pay one-third of a gold mina.

167. If any one strike the body of a man higher in rank than he, he shall receive sixty blows with an ox-whip in public.

168. If a free-born man strike the body of another free-born man or equal rank, he shall pay one gold mina.

169. If a freed man strike the body of another freed man, he shall pay ten shekels in money.

170. If the slave of a freed man strike the body of a freed man, his ear shall be cut off.

171. If during a quarrel one man strike another and wound him, then he shall swear, "I did not injure him wittingly," and pay the physicians.

172. If the man die of his wound, he shall swear similarly, and if he (the deceased) was a free-born man, he shall pay half a mina in money.

173. If he was a freed man, he shall pay one-third of a mina.

174. If a man strike a free-born woman so that she lose her unborn child, he shall pay ten shekels for her loss.

175. If the woman die, his daughter shall be put to death.

176. If a woman of the free class lose her child by a blow, he shall pay five shekels in money.

177. If this woman die, he shall pay half a mina.

178. If he strike the maid-servant of a man, and she lose her child, he shall pay two shekels in money.

179. If this maid-servant die, he shall pay one-third of a mina.

180. If a physician make a large incision with an operating knife and cure it, or if he open a tumor (over the eye) with an operating knife, and saves the eye, he shall receive ten shekels in money.

181. If the patient be a freed man, he receives five shekels.

182. If he be the slave of some one, his owner shall give the physician two shekels.

183. If a physician make a large incision with the operating knife, and kill him, or open a tumor with the operating knife, and cut out the eye, his hands shall be cut off.

184. If a physician make a large incision in the slave of a freed man, and kill him, he shall replace the slave with another slave.

185. If he had opened a tumor with the operating knife, and put out his eye, he shall pay half his value.

186. If a physician heal the broken bone or diseased soft part of a man, the patient shall pay the physician five shekels in money.

187. If he were a freed man he shall pay three shekels.

188. If he were a slave his owner shall pay the physician two shekels.

189. If a veterinary surgeon perform a serious operation on an ass or an ox, and cure it, the owner shall pay the surgeon one-sixth of a shekel as a fee.

190. If he perform a serious operation on an ass or ox, and kill it, he shall pay the owner one-fourth of its value.

191. If a barber, without the knowledge of his master, cut the sign of a slave on a slave not to be sold, the hands of this barber shall be cut off.

192. If any one deceive a barber, and have him mark a slave not for sale with the sign of a slave, he shall be put to death, and buried in his house. The barber shall swear: "I did not mark him wittingly," and shall be guiltless.

193. If a builder build a house for some one and complete it, he shall give him a fee of two shekels in money for each sar of surface.

194. 229 If a builder build a house for some one, and does not construct it properly, and the house which he built fall in and kill its owner, then that builder shall be put to death.

195. If it kill the son of the owner the son of that builder shall be put to death.

196. If it kill a slave of the owner, then he shall pay slave for slave to the owner of the house.

197. If it ruin goods, he shall make compensation for all that has been ruined, and inasmuch as he did not construct properly

this house which he built and it fell, he shall re-erect the house from his own means.

198. If a builder build a house for some one, even though he has not yet completed it; if then the walls seem toppling, the builder must make the walls solid from his own means.

199. If a shipbuilder build a boat of sixty gur for a man, he shall pay him a fee of two shekels in money.

200.   If a shipbuilder build a boat for some one, and do not make it tight, if during that same year that boat is sent away and suffers injury, the shipbuilder shall take the boat apart and put it together tight at his own expense. The tight boat he shall give to the boat owner.

201. If a man rent his boat to a sailor, and the sailor is careless, and the boat is wrecked or goes aground, the sailor shall give the owner of the boat another boat as compensation.

202. If a man hire a sailor and his boat, and provide it with corn, clothing, oil and dates, and other things of the kind needed for fitting it: if the sailor is careless, the boat is wrecked, and its contents ruined, then the sailor shall compensate for the boat which was wrecked and all in it that he ruined.

203. If a sailor wreck any one's ship, but saves it, he shall pay the half of its value in money.

204. If a man hire a sailor, he shall pay him six gur of corn per year.

205. If a merchantman run against a ferryboat, and wreck it, the master of the ship that was wrecked shall seek justice before

God; the master of the merchantman, which wrecked the ferryboat, must compensate the owner for the boat and all that he ruined.

206.   If any one impresses an ox for forced labor, he shall pay one-third of a mina in money.

207. If any one hire oxen for a year, he shall pay four gur of corn for plow-oxen.

208. As rent of herd cattle he shall pay three gur of corn to the owner.

209. If any one hire an ox or an ass, and a lion kill it in the field, the loss is upon its owner.

210. If any one hire oxen, and kill them by bad treatment or blows, he shall compensate the owner, oxen for oxen.

211. If a man hire an ox, and he break its leg or cut the ligament of its neck, he shall compensate the owner with ox for ox.

212. If any one hire an ox, and put out its eye, he shall pay the owner one-half of its value.

213. If any one hire an ox, and break off a horn, or cut off its tail, or hurt its muzzle, he shall pay one-fourth of its value in money.

214. If any one hire an ox, and God strike it that it die, the man who hired it shall swear by God and be considered guiltless.

215. If while an ox is passing on the street (market) some one push it, and kill it, the owner can set up no claim in the suit (against the hirer).

216. If an ox be a goring ox, and it shown that he is a gorer, and he do not bind his horns, or fasten the ox up, and the ox gore a free-born man and kill him, the owner shall pay one-half a mina in money.

217. If he kill a man's slave, he shall pay one-third of a mina.

218. If any one agree with another to tend his field, give him seed, entrust a yoke of oxen to him, and bind him to cultivate the field, if he steal the corn or plants, and take them for himself, his hands shall be hewn off.

219. If he take the seed-corn for himself, and do not use the yoke of oxen, he shall compensate him for the amount of the seed-corn.

220. If he sublet the man's yoke of oxen or steal the seed-corn, planting nothing in the field, he shall be convicted, and for each one hundred gan he shall pay sixty gur of corn.

221. If his community will not pay for him, then he shall be placed in that field with the cattle (at work).

222. If any one hire a field laborer, he shall pay him eight gur of corn per year.

223. If any one hire an ox-driver, he shall pay him six gur of corn per year.

224. If any one steal a water-wheel from the field, he shall pay five shekels in money to its owner.

225. If any one steal a shadduf (used to draw water from the river or canal) or a plow, he shall pay three shekels in money.

226. If any one hire a herdsman for cattle or sheep, he shall pay him eight gur of corn per annum.

227. If any one, a cow or a sheep . . .

228. If he kill the cattle or sheep that were given to him, he shall compensate the owner with cattle for cattle and sheep for sheep.

229. If a herdsman, to whom cattle or sheep have been entrusted for watching over, and who has received his wages as agreed upon, and is satisfied, diminish the number of the cattle or sheep, or make the increase by birth less, he shall make good the increase or profit which was lost in the terms of settlement.

230. If a herdsman, to whose care cattle or sheep have been entrusted, be guilty of fraud and make false returns of the natural increase, or sell them for money, then shall he be convicted and pay the owner ten times the loss.

231. If the animal be killed in the stable by God (an accident), or if a lion kill it, the herdsman shall declare his innocence before God, and the owner bears the accident in the stable.

232. If the herdsman overlook something, and an accident happen in the stable, then the herdsman is at fault for the accident which he has caused in the stable, and he must compensate the owner for the cattle or sheep.

233. If any one hire an ox for threshing, the amount of the hire is twenty ka of corn.

234. If he hire an ass for threshing, the hire is twenty ka of corn.

235. If he hire a young animal for threshing, the hire is ten ka of corn.

236. If any one hire oxen, cart and driver, he shall pay one hundred and eighty ka of corn per day.

237. If any one hire a cart alone, he shall pay forty ka of corn per day.

238. If any one hire a day laborer, he shall pay him from the New Year until the fifth month (April to August, when days are long and the work hard) six gerahs in money per day; from the sixth month to the end of the year he shall give him five gerahs per day.

239. If any one hire a skilled artizan, he shall pay as wages of the . . . five gerahs, as wages of the potter five gerahs, of a tailor five gerahs, of . . . gerahs, . . . of a ropemaker four gerahs, of . . . gerahs, of a mason . . . gerahs per day.

240. If any one hire a ferryboat, he shall pay three gerahs in money per day.

241. If he hire a freight-boat, he shall pay two and one-half gerahs per day.

242. If any one hire a ship of sixty gur, he shall pay one-sixth of a shekel in money as its hire per day.

243. If any one buy a male or female slave, and before a month has elapsed the benu-disease be developed, he shall return the slave to the seller, and receive the money which he had paid.

244. If any one buy a male or female slave, and a third party claim it, the seller is liable for the claim.

245. If while in a foreign country a man buy a male or female slave belonging to another of his own country; if when he return home the owner of the male or female slave recognize it: if the male or female slave be a native of the country, he shall give them back without any money.

246. If they are from another country, the buyer shall declare the amount of money paid therefor to the merchant, and keep the male or female slave.

247. If a slave say to his master: "You are not my master," if they convict him his master shall cut off his ear.

Questions

How far can you go if you're afraid to take the first step?

What will you learn in life if you're terrified of making mistakes?

Would life be an adventure if we all knew our fate?

What can be conquered that's not confronted?

Why should I conform to the norm if the norm is a lowered conscience mind state?

Why do problems always arise in dark places?

Will there ever be understanding among the many human races?

What is the purpose of life?

What should I do when the rain showers of life are abrasive?

Will my life force sustain the life of others?

Have I ever felt empty?

Why Do we all adore fortune and fame?

If the way the world behaves depends on how or if we look at it, what can reality really mean?

So many Questions about life, statements and claims. The one thing for sure. No one's life is the same.

Quotes By Napoleon Hill

"The starting point of all achievement is desire. Keep this constant in mind. Weak desire brings weak results, just as small fires make a small amount of heat."

"You are the master of your destiny. You can influence, direct and control your own environment. You can make your life what you want it to be."

"Before success comes in any man's life, he is sure to meet with much temporary defeat, and, perhaps, some failure. When defeat overtakes a man, the easiest and most logical thing to do is to quit. That is exactly what the majority of men do. More than five hundred of the most successful men this country has ever known told the author their greatest success came just one step beyond the point at which defeat had overtaken them."

"Set your mid on a definite goal and observe how quickly the whole world stands aside to let you pass."

"The way of success is the way of continuous pursuit of knowledge."

"Happiness is found in doing, Not merely possessing."

"Every adversity, every failure, every heartbreak, carries with it the seed of an equal or greater benefit."

"An educated man is not, necessarily, one who has an abundance of general or specialized knowledge. An educated man is one who has so developed the faculties of his mind that he may acquire anything he wants, or its equivalent, without violating the rights of others."

"More gold has been mined from the mine of men than from the earth itself."

"To win the big stakes in this changed world, you must catch the spirit of the great pioneers of the past, whose dreams have given to civilization all that it has value, the spirit that serves as the life-blood of our own country-Your opportunity and mine, to develop and market our talents."

"I will eliminate hatred, envy, jealousy, selfishness, and cynicism, by developing love for all humanity, because I know that a negative attitude toward others can never bring success. I will cause others to believe in me, because I will believe in them, and in myself."

"Opinions are the cheapest commodities on earth. Everyone has a flock of opinions ready to be wished upon anyone who will accept them. If you are influenced by "opinions" when you reach decisions, you will not succeed in any undertaking."

"Put your foot upon the neck of fear of criticism by reaching a decision not to worry about what other people think, do, or say."

"There is a difference between wishing for a thing and being ready to receive it. No one is ready for a thing, until he believes he can acquire it. The state of mind must be belief, not mere hope or wish. Open-mindedness is essential for belief."

"Those who succeed in an outstanding way seldom do so before the age of 40. More often, they do not strike their real pace until they are well beyond the age of 50."

"Remember too, that all who succeed in life get off to a bad start and pass through many heartbreaking struggles before the arrive. The turning point in the lives of those who succeed usually comes at some moment of crisis through which they are introduced to their other selves."

"If – and this is the greatest of them all- I had the courage to see myself as I really am, I would find out what is wrong with me, and correct it, then I might have a chance to profit by my mistakes and learn something from the experience of others, for I know that there is something wrong with me, or I would now be where I would have been if I had spent more time analyzing my weaknesses, and less time building alibis to cover them."

Definitions

- **Spatial Cognition**- Is a branch of cognitive psychology that studies how people acquire and use knowledge about their environment to determine where they are, how to obtain resources, and how to find their way home.
- **Inner man**- the spiritual or intellectual part of a man.
- **De ambitu**- of devious methods of securing a position as through bribery.
- **Deamplior gratia**- of more abundant or more full grace.
- **De bene esse**- accept for now.
- **Law of Cognition**- a person is what he or she thinks.
- **Law of exposure**- the mind will think most about what it is most exposed to.
- **Culture**- a pattern of ways and means by which a group or society strives to fulfill its basic needs.
- **Empirical**- based on experience, experiment or observation.
- **Fiat money**- paper money that in contrast to hard currency is not backed by reserves but instead derives its value from Government regulation or law declaring it legal tender.

- **Real money-**money that has metallic or other intrinsic value as distinguished from paper currency, checks, and drafts.
- **Smart money-**funds held by sophisticated, usually large investors who are capable of minimizing risks and maximizing profits.
- **Extrovert-**a gregarious and unreserved person.
- **Introvert-**a reserved person.
- **Damnant quod non intelligunt- they condemn what they don't know**
- **Conscious-**the upper level of the mental life of which a person is aware.
- **Pathos-**a quality that evokes pity or sadness.
- **Ethos-**the characteristic spirit of a culture, era or community as manifested in its beliefs and aspirations.
- **Logos-**the word of God, or principle of divine reason and creative order.
- **Ego-**a person's sense of self-esteem or self-importance.
- **SuperEgo-**the part of a person's mind that acts as a self-critical conscience, reflecting social standards learned from parents and teachers.
- **Id-**the part of the mind in which innate instinctive impulses and primary processes are manifest.

There are 7 dominant spheres of influence: movies, music, television, books, internet, law, and family. The 2nd tier of influences are: schools, peers, newspapers, radio, and business
George Barna

"This above all: to thine own self be true, and it must follow, as the night the day, thou canst not then be false to any man"
Hamlet

https://www.Facebook.com/Jerrod.biglow

Printed in the United States
by Baker & Taylor Publisher Services